INK FROM THE PEN
A Prison Memoir

Mark Olmsted

Ink from the Pen
@2017 by Mark Olmsted

Book Cover Design by: Sandra Moreano
Interior Design by: Sandra Moreano

Published by:
Nuance Titles
Los Angeles CA 90027
www.nuancetitles.com

ISBN-13: 978-0692784143
ISBN-10: 0692784144

Note:Everything in this memoir happened. Some names
and identifying details have been changed to protect the
privacy of individuals.

for
Sandra
sister and muse extraordinaire

CONTENTS

161
Part Three
Redwood

Afterwords

Preface

I have been various kinds of writer all my life, but only managed to produce my first book quite accidentally. It began in Los Angeles Men's County Jail, when I thought I was just writing a lot of letters, mostly to my sister, Sandra. After about a month of this, she told me they were really good, and she wanted to type up a letter every day and post it on a blog she'd create for me. (I didn't even know what a blog was back in 2004, but when she explained, of course I enthusiastically said yes.)

Knowing that I was writing for an audience, even a small one, was transformational. It was as if the men I was incarcerated with sensed they were on stage, and produced a little play for me every day. I just had to report what I was seeing. And after the lost years of drug addiction, it felt like nothing short of a miracle to be writing again.

Of course, a blog is not a book, but it did give me the raw material to reshape into what you are about to read. One of the biggest reasons it took so long was the prologue. I kept trying to write explaining how I got to prison in the first place. Unexpectedly, I found that "before" time much more painful to revisit than my time behind bars, because it was so inextricably linked not only to my addiction and criminality, but the 25 years of fear and grief that came from living with AIDS during the very worst years of it. Instead, I wrote screenplays, essays, poetry, fiction, you name it. Finally, I accepted that the sequel would have to come before the prequel, and I published, *Ink from the Pen: A Prison Memoir*.

When word-of-mouth didn't quite work as I'd hoped, I wrote a piece for Medium entitled: "Breaking Brokebad: A

True Gay Crime Story I Never Would Have Believed If I Hadn't Lived It." And rather spontaneously, I tweeted it to a reporter for GQ whose work I liked, Nathaniel Penn, with the note: "Why don't you do a story about me?" To my everlasting surprise, he responded immediately in the affirmative. GQ flew him down to meet me. A photographer soon followed. In the next months, we did follow-up interviews, and he reached out extensively to my family and friends for background. He wrote, edited, rewrote, re-edited. The piece was ready to go in the Spring of 2018, but the Goddesses seemed intent on teaching me (yet again) that the secret of life is to accept those things which are beyond your control, like editorial changes at major magazines as they are forced to reinvent themselves in a changing media landscape.

But Nate did successfully navigate those roiling waters, and his insightful and beautifully written article, *The Man Who Wouldn't Die,* went up on GQ.com in late April, 2019. In fact, most of you probably discovered this book because you read the article first. And having done so, you probably understand why telling the story of my downfall myself proved so daunting to me.

I would have been too unreliable a narrator of my own story. I would have rearranged memories, justified behavior, conveniently omitted those bits from my past where I came off quite badly. All forgivable, even expected, in most creative non-fiction, but not in an autobiographical memoir about a consummate liar, forger, and successful faker of his own death. I needed an impeccable journalist and a phalanx of fact-checkers to make my stranger-than-fiction truth believable.

If you are coming first to the book, reading the article is by no means a prerequisite to enjoying the next 260 or so pages. But considering GQ doesn't have a paywall, and archives their articles indefinitely, do know that the answers to all your questions concerning what I did and how and why I did it are readily available with just a few clicks.

This book is not the story of getting to prison; it is the story of being there. I was an educated, gay, HIV+, 45-year-old man in a situation for which nothing in my experience had prepared me.

Or so I thought.

I would discover that creativity is one of the most powerful survival tools there is.

PART ONE
LOS ANGELES COUNTY JAIL

In Pieces

The first time I was arrested, I knew that my drug-dealing confederates would raise my bail within 72 hours, and they did. The second time, when I was denied bond, one of my most immediate concerns was that there was no way I'd be at home to answer my phone the next time my mother called. While I sweated it out in a jail cell, sure enough, she left two messages on my machine and began to sound concerned by the third. I *always* called back — that was one of my rules. Being a dealer and an addict was no excuse for being a shitty son, and this was one way I convinced myself I wasn't a shitty son.

My "roommates" (hangers-on that I let use my second bedroom) knew about this pact that I'd made with myself, and so they finally picked up the phone.

To say that my mother was shocked by the news that I'd been arrested would be accurate — but wholly inadequate. My mother's sister Francoise later used the French word *morcelée* to describe the effect on my mother, "cut into tiny little pieces." That description still haunts me.

Mom immediately called my sister Sandra, who is one year older than me. At the time, she was living in Albuquerque with her husband Alex, an ENT surgeon. Her eldest son, Keir, was in his second year at NYU Film School (which I had attended 25 years prior). Her daughter Daniella was just finishing high school. My sister had known I did drugs, but however secretive my lifestyle, dealing meth was a completely different realm entirely. To her, it was barely conceivable that she was hearing the words that she was hearing. I had not just lied a little — I had lied *a lot*. I had lied prodigiously.

14

My other sister Erica had just adopted her second child, so it would have been a nightmare if the task of handling this crisis had landed on her shoulders. Thankfully, Sandra had the wherewithal to hire a lawyer. I also put her in touch with the one friend of mine whose wholesomeness would allow her to imagine I was not as far gone as I was.

Derek was an Ivy League-educated professional with whom I had regular meth-fueled sexcapades. But he kept our taboo relationship compartmentalized from the rest of his life. In communicating with my sister, he gave absolutely no outward indication that he had been involved in any darker goings-on. (Later, she perplexedly asked, "Derek didn't do crystal, did he?" It was just too hard to imagine this blond Yalie — a refugee from a family of Seventh-Day Adventists — in the sling above my bed.)

Except for one visit from my lawyer and one from Derek, I had little contact with anyone during the first ten days after my arrest. This was because, in a misguided attempt to gain sympathy from the judge and get sentenced to a lockdown rehab instead of prison, I told the psych intake coordinator down at Twin Towers that, yes, I did have thoughts of suicide.

It was a stupid move.

Twenty minutes later my name was called out. Having been in a nightmarish holding cell for hours, crammed with 20 other inmates, then cuffed to a bench during medical intake, it was my first moment of hope since my arrest. "Ah," I thought, "I'm finally going to be moved into a dorm." I even had a fleeting fantasy I was going to be released.

But as the guard elaborately chained me up like a prisoner at Guantanamo Bay, the initial feeling of relief gave way to dread. This didn't look good at all.

The guard who escorted me wouldn't explain why he was taking away my glasses, but later I found out that those truly intent on committing suicide have been known to break their lenses and then slit their wrists with the shards.

I was put into a holding cage next to a very handsome young Cuban in an adjoining enclosure. His name was Aldo. We were both in veritable straight jackets, separated by a wire mesh, but at least we could talk and swap the requisite what-are-you-in-here-for stories.

The insanity of my addiction was of the slow-motion variety, unfolding over the long term with an elaborate scaffolding of rationalization. I was no typical tweaker — the rent was always paid, the bathroom kept clean, the refrigerator well-stocked. This was how I convinced myself that I used meth as Hemingway used alcohol — in excess, perhaps, but as a substance that nonetheless enhanced my life overall.

When even I had to admit this was a bit of a stretch, I down-shifted into seeing it as a kind of unfortunate necessity; a medication I needed to function, just like I needed my HIV meds to keep the virus under control.

Aldo was an addict of the less restrained variety. He binged for days at a time, wreaking increasing havoc in his wake. It took me a while to understand this, though, because at first he so vividly painted a supposedly faithless, money-stealing boyfriend as the villain of his story. Eventually, I parsed enough details to realize that charges of aggravated mayhem against Aldo were in all likelihood completely justified. Most damning of all, his intimate knowledge of how to make a PB&J soufflé with the contents of our lunch was evidence that this was not his first time at the Central Jail rodeo. (This mutant confection basically involved shmushing the peanut butter and jelly sandwich in a plastic bag until it was an amorphous, multi-colored lump. It tasted exactly the same, but fashioning it felt right out of an old MacGyver episode, and it was something to do.)

As a dealer, I had cut off more than a few customers like Aldo. Later on, I would learn in 12-step meetings that it was far more common for someone to get sober because his supplier suggested it than because his doctor did. "When your dealer tells you

you've got a problem," the share would go, "then you *know* you've got a problem."

Eventually Aldo and I were taken to different cells in multi-leveled pods that constituted the wing of the jail where they put suicide risks. This was a modern addition to the aging main facility; clean white rooms with glass doors so that no at-risk inmate could make much of an attempt at killing himself without being seen by the cameras. Stacked above and below each other in widely angled arcs, we couldn't see each other, but the muffled cacophony was constant and vaguely nightmarish, as if *King Lear* and The Snake Pit were being concurrently rehearsed in adjoining buildings.

Across from us was a single TV, mocking us really, as we couldn't hear it well; and if you'd had your glasses taken away as I had, you couldn't see much of it either. Still, I grew to be grateful for the station on which the TV channel was generally set. It showed mainly black sit-coms marked by such an emphatic exaggerated acting style ("oh, girl, no you didn't!") that made it easier to follow the story, or at least invent one to go along with it. I would listen under the door to try to make out a few snatches of dialogue, then quickly peer up at the action through the thick glass, squinting. It made for pitifully inadequate entertainment.

For seven straight days, there was absolutely nothing to do. No reading material was allowed — later I found out that this was in reaction to an inmate who tried to commit suicide by stuffing pages of a book down his throat.

The worst of it was not having a toothbrush — a precious item I will never again take for granted. Even the toilet paper was doled out by a porter who only slid the sheets as needed under the door. Later, a guard would come by to flush the commode from the outside with a special key.

I took to staring out of the slit that constituted the exterior window, yielding a most unappetizing view of industrial Los Angeles. In the distance snaked a freeway — the I-10, I think —

and I concentrated on projecting my consciousness into the cars, imagining I might make the drivers feel a barely perceptible but not unpleasant zing. (To this day, when I drive by, I look up and try to send a zing back up there, just in case someone like me is also staring out, desperate not to be forgotten.)

I had not understood during my admission that status reevaluations occurred only after you'd been under watch for at least a week. After the third day of stupefying boredom, I figured that if I could just explain that I wasn't *really* suicidal, they would let me into one of the special gay dorms that Los Angeles County offered for our protection.

Twice a day, a severe Korean nurse would dispense my HIV medication, trailed by a bored guard. She wasn't the Chatty Cathy type and completely ignored my pleas to see an intake officer or psychiatrist. She would just open the door, watch me take my pills, and move on without a word. On the fourth day I got pissed at not getting the slightest acknowledgement and blocked the closing door with my foot.

"I need to see someone about being moved!" I insisted.

The guard that accompanied her was delighted — finally, something to do! He enthusiastically summoned backup, and a trio of officers moved into my cell, menacing me with their nightsticks. I went into full apology-mode.

"I'm sorry. I don't know why I did that. I was wrong."

"Damn right, you were," said one officer. "You wanted to take something from her; well, we're going to take something from you."

This was a strange thing to say, as I had tried no such thing. But the accusation served to justify the punishment, I guess. They made me take off my prison oranges, leaving me in nothing but underwear and socks. That was really all they could do, as I had no privileges to revoke, and the suddenly useful overhead cameras would have made thwacking me over the head problematic.

The wing was cooled to a ridiculously low 66 degrees or so,

and in the aftermath of my impulsive *Norma Rae* stance, I huddled under my thin sheet, fighting fugues of anxiety in which I imagined a Kafkaesque future wherein I was indefinitely lost and forgotten in the system.

The next day, a female corrections officer was assigned to accompany the nurse, and she inquired where my clothes had gone. When I told her, she rolled her eyes at the zealousness of her co-workers and, after Pill Call was over, came back with a new uniform. She also let me out to take a shower and use the phone. I called my sister and asked her to see if my lawyer could get me moved. Sandra told me she'd try, but in the meantime had sent me some books.

I was neither lost nor forgotten.

A year or so after I got out, I read my sister's journal entries about what she was going through during this period. I do not have the courage to ask her for the passages to repeat them here. Suffice to say, the blows spared me by those guards might as well have landed on her. Poor Sandra was sleepless, disoriented, infuriated, and worried sick, but she unfailingly kept her cool each and every time I called.

Buoyed by my brief sortie from the cell and the kindness of the guard, I decided to use the time purposefully. At first I tried to meditate, but all I ended up contemplating was the futility of trying. I'd been off meth a week, and was probably going to prison. The notion of stilling my mind was laughable.

I had no pen, no paper, nothing to read. There wasn't much left to do but talk to myself. It wasn't a very original thing to do in this neck of the woods, of course, where one could hear snippets of incoherent soliloquies from every pod in the wing. But I'm pretty sure I was the only one who began speaking in French.

This would have been remarkable if I didn't speak French, but I am indeed quite fluent. What was remarkable was that I wasn't articulating any ideas that were consciously my own. The words seemed to be coming from an uncle who'd died 44 years before, almost to the day.

Roger was my mother's adored older brother, a brilliant anthropology and sociology professor in Montpellier, France. He had been in the French Resistance, and after the war married his college sweetheart, Anne-Marie. They'd had five children, the last in 1958, a month before I was born on the other side of the Atlantic.

In 1960, he got up from the dinner table, kissed his children one by one, and then layed down, complaining of fatigue. This wasn't unusual, as he'd struggled with chronic nephritis. But no one had any idea how impaired his kidney actually was.

When his wife went to check on him an hour later, she found him dead.

My mother, in the United States with five of her own young children, was devastated. She cried every day for a year. Although I was not even two, I have always been sure that I was deeply affected by it. I grew up fascinated by my uncle, certain I would have been much closer to him than I was to my own father.

What Roger explained to me in my cell was that the soul remains unreincarnated into another being until the very moment the last person to have had contact with you when you were alive, dies. So if your youngest daughter lives to be 95 and survives all of her siblings, then your soul is released only when she herself passes away. That is why there is truth to the cliché that someone who has died remains alive in one's heart. The soul stays tethered to the last human consciousness that has felt it personally.

I have little doubt that this unexpected epiphany was fabricated by my imagination, but even on that score alone, it was significant. Meth had long crowded out most thoughts unrelated to the physical here and now. Conjuring up my Uncle Roger represented something metaphorical — a door reopening to spiritual experience.

I didn't know it yet, but that week I began to learn, in baby steps taken one hour at a time, that I could be alone with myself, that I did not have to constantly regulate my emotional and physical state with a drug or a relationship or money. This almost banal life lesson had long ago been unlearned in the haze of my addiction.

Seven days into this purest of rock bottoms, I was taken to meet a personable but cautiously correct young psychiatrist who was probably in as much shock that she'd ended up working in a prison as I was being held in one. I told her I wasn't at all suicidal, and she signed me out with a kind but well-rehearsed smile.

As I was let out of my cell, some mail and a book were placed in my hand. The book was from my older brother Steve, a rather dry anthology of artists responding to AIDS. He meant well, but it was the last thing I wanted to read. I wanted *Gone with the Wind* or *War and Peace* or a Stephen King doorstop. Anything that could serve as a conduit to another world, not something that reminded me of why, once upon a time, I never thought I'd make it to age 40.

Just at that moment, before I'd taken more than a step or two, I saw none other than Aldo. He'd been in the cell next to me all of this time. Through the glass, he told me he was in for another week, casting his eyes lustfully at my reading material. In a stroke of inspiration, I took the paperback my brother had sent me, splayed it open face down, and managed to slide it under the glass door. I don't know how I did this without being seen by the guard, but I think that several of us were being moved, and he was busy unlocking another cell. Aldo pulled the book through to his side and threw it under the sheet of his bed with the expert speed of an inmate who understood that surviving in prison required seizing unexpected opportunities. Aldo mouthed, "thank you!" with an expression of gratitude on his face as soulful as a cripple at Lourdes who's just been able to throw away his crutches.

Calendar

As my troupe of co-transferees followed the guard to our new quarters, there was a real swagger in my step. You'd think someone who had forged his own death certificate on more than one occasion would find the rush of sneaking a book under a door rather small potatoes, but in prison, the little triumphs felt very big indeed.

At the same time, I had given away my only book, and dreaded the possibility of having nothing to read. For ten years, even during the worst of my addiction, I'd always had *The New York Times* delivered to my doorstep. I would peruse it in bits during the day — with morning coffee, or while having an evening cocktail. It was a ritual I clung to as part of the fiction that if I was a news junkie, this disqualified me from being the other kind of junkie.

Around most corners there was usually a desk where an officer could eat lunch or do paperwork. As we approached one such station, I spotted a copy of the *Los Angeles Times* — just disheveled enough to indicate it had already been read. We had to stop just then, and I found myself tantalizingly close to this treasure. I strained to see a headline in the pile, but the sections lay too haphazardly upon one another. I cursed the gods. Didn't they know a week in solitary felt like six months anywhere else? How could they be so cruel?

We got the signal to move again, and I knew the newspaper would soon be out of reach. Still cocky from my impromptu smuggling operation to Aldo, my hand shot out like a lizard's tongue, and in a split second Section F was under my shirt.

I might have gotten away with it if the porter — an inmate with some responsibilities outside of his cell — hadn't seen a suspicious movement from the corner of his eye. If something important went missing on his watch — say, a pen — he could lose his privileges.

A minute or so later, as we rounded a corner, I suddenly found myself up against a wall, legs spread apart, my arm yanked up my back. Oddly, I didn't even panic.

"Did you steal something, inmate?" barked the guard.

"Yes, sir!" I admitted.

"And what did you steal?"

"A newspaper ... I'm sorry!"

The cop could feel my utter lack of resistance, and relaxed the position of my arm. He had me turn around, and I handed him the offending contraband.

"The *Calendar* section," I added meekly.

This caused laughter down the line, and even the guard was amused.

"You do know you're in jail, right?"

I nodded, dumbly.

"And stealing could get you in serious trouble?"

More dumb nodding.

"So why would you steal a goddamn newspaper?"

Everyone seemed to lean forward, genuinely curious.

"I just wanted to know what was going on in the world, sir."

For just a moment, you could almost hear the rustle of air as heads shook back and forth in grave, astonished unison. This was simply not a situation anyone had ever come across — an inmate who was willing to risk the wrath of a nightstick just to find out who'd won the New Hampshire primary?

The truth seemed to disarm the officer, who rolled his eyes as if to indicate that he'd finally seen everything. Using the paper as his baton, he gestured us forward.

I was immensely relieved, of course, and appalled by my own brazen recklessness. On the other hand, it was all I could do to not ask the guard if I could still have the newspaper.

I had hoped we were being taken directly to the dorms, where I knew I would find a friend who had been arrested a month before. But it was Friday, and that kind of processing would have to wait until Monday. Several of us had to spend the weekend in what appeared to be a converted storage room, repurposed due to overcrowding. I lay on a thin mattress, wondering how I was going to survive two more days wandering parched in a desert without the written word.

An inmate who had witnessed the newspaper incident sat, unbidden, on my bunk.

"Well, Poindexter," he said. "You are either the bravest or the dumbest fuck I have ever met."

It was hard to argue that I was the former. I didn't even bother trying to explain. What was I going to say, that my idea of hell was waiting for a bus without something to read?

Just then, there was a slight commotion at the wire mesh separating us from the hallway. Someone on the other side of the bars was trying to get my attention.

"Hey, you!"

"Me?"

"Yeah."

It was the porter, a short, sinewy kid with the scruffy energy of a born hustler.

"Here!"

He was pushing something through the slot into my hands. It was the entire weekend edition of the newspaper, which he'd evidently retrieved and reconstituted. My mouth fell open. By the time I could muster a thank you, my paperboy had disappeared as fast as a genie whisked back into his bottle, wish granted.

I have often wondered about his motives. He may have feared being perceived as a snitch for having ratted me out to the officer, or he may have just wanted to show respect to a fellow risk taker. Most likely, he simply found it a useful survival strategy to be owed a favor.

At the time, it only felt like kindness.

I danced a jig right there, offering sections of this unexpected bounty to whoever was as hungry for distraction as I was. Then I settled on my bunk, gleeful as a 5-year-old girl wearing a brand new dress on the first day of school.

Such moments of reprieve in prison would be consistent only in one particular characteristic — their complete unpredictability.

Denizens

That Monday, we were called to be interviewed individually by one of the deputies who supervised the K-11 dorms. Their job was to make sure no one was faking being gay to avoid the far more violent regular dorms, although plenty who'd learned the names of a few gay bars routinely got through. I passed with flying colors, of course, and the kindly and avuncular "Deputy Mike" actually took me personally to the property room to retrieve my glasses.

He assigned me to the least hectic of the three gay dorms, 5100, which consisted of a cavernous room with about 75 bunk beds. We were watched from above, quite literally, by in a guard box that stretched into the adjoining dorms, so that one officer could go back and forth supervising all of them. An inmate "house-mouse" was appointed by the corrections officers to oversee each room.

As soon as I was given my bunk assignment, I scoured the dorm for the man who'd been my meth supplier. He'd been arrested the month before. Larry was actually something of a friend, at least by the standards of lower companionship to which I'd become accustomed. He was 64, a Vietnam vet, and the father of a few grown sons. He was as thin as a folding chair and looked and sounded like a wizened Okie farmer. He'd done a few substantial stretches of time in prison, but every time he got out, he drifted back into the life of a dealer, less for the money than for the handsome Latino boys who gladly hung around him for the free meth.

I was incredibly relieved to find him, if only to borrow some real toothpaste, as the powder the county supplied tasted like detergent. Larry explained to me that every week we filled out an order form for food and toiletries, which took a week to be delivered. You could order up to $200 worth of items. Derek had deposited some money in my account a few days before, but my timing was bad, as I'd arrived to the dorm literally just hours after the cut-off point for submitting the next week's order. Seeing my distress, Larry put together a care package for me out of his own supplies.

He was a little embarrassed by my gratitude.

"Hang on, hang on, don't go crying on me. It's just a few soups and some chips. You'll pay me back."

As if I could ever.

The black friends I made at County stand out in my memory because later on, when I was no longer in the gay dorms, it would be much more difficult to reach across racial lines. There was JoJo, a basketball fanatic who loved hairy men and came on to me constantly; Cooley, a natural clown I correctly guessed to be the youngest boy in a large family of girls; and Undertaker, who gave me one of the best haircuts I ever had with just a comb and a smuggled razor. I paid him with packages of ramen soup (along with stamps, the other main currency of prison).

Undertaker was the first black gay man I'd met who lived on the down-low. He was cagey about how he got his name, but it struck me as pretty smart marketing for anyone incarcerated and seeking to build a rep without having to actually be violent.

With me he was charming and affable, and I certainly didn't mind staring at his chiseled body as he clipped my hair. The effect would have been complete had his looks not been marred by missing teeth. This was a pretty common look in prison. Gone, it seemed, were the glory days of the '70s, when supposedly men would violate their parole just to finish their dental work.

Jeff was a good-looking 28-year-old with big blue eyes that were always on the lookout for a younger boyfriend. What made him so original was an absolute passion for the poet John Milton. Jeff would recite entire passages of *Paradise Lost* from a dog-eared copy sent to him by the Jesuit brothers who ran the orphanage in which he'd been raised — the setting of his own tragic saga.

Jeff had been taken from his mentally ill mother when he was 1-year-old, then fostered by a young couple who'd intended to adopt him. A few months later, they returned him to the orphanage instead. Years later, the psychiatrist would tell Jeff his diagnosis was "affective bonding disorder." I shuddered to hear anyone describe himself that way. I knew such a syndrome existed, but it seemed the sort of immutable trait that someone never would admit to if they really had it, like being a sociopath. I wondered if perhaps he just wanted sympathy, since clearly anyone who loved the classical poets clearly had a taste for melodrama.

Then he told me about the crime that had landed him here. In a fit of jealous rage, Jeff had beaten a boyfriend into a coma with a bowling pin.

The crime seemed so out of sync with this young man who hoped to one day teach English Literature that I couldn't conjure up enough fear to reject the offer of his top bunk. Besides, I had just laid my hand on an ink pen, and my current bunk was woefully close to the guard booth. Jeff's corner location would allow me to use my treasure unobserved.

Occasionally he would ask me with a childlike expression whether I thought his comatose ex was going to die, looking at me with the trusting eyes of someone who imagined that my powerless guessing about that likelihood would have some bearing on its outcome. I had little trouble seeing in my mind's eye a ten-month-old standing in his crib, looking out hopefully with those same eyes at a mother who found herself unable to hold her own child.

He would often pace the dorm late at night, riven by regret and horror at what he'd done, praying that assault with a deadly weapon wouldn't become a murder charge. Exhausting himself, he tended to catch up on sleep in the afternoon, letting one of my sheets serve as a curtain over his bottom bunk.

One day it was my turn to sweep our section of the dorm, and I accidentally touched the metal frame of the bed with the broom. He swept open the sheet, and with barely controlled fury, warned that I seriously needed to respect his sleep. The unspoken "or else" hung in the air, and my protestations that it was completely unintentional provoked a glare so menacing that I went to the "house mouse" that afternoon and got a move authorized.

Later, Jeff came to me crestfallen.

"I wouldn't hurt you" he insisted. "I'm just grouchy when I'm awakened like that."

"And I told you it was a total accident. Listen, Jeff, I like you, really, I do. For God's sake, you're memorizing the Romantic poets in jail. But, dude, you have a temper, and it scares me. And I'm not going to be more scared than I already am just by being here."

I was an anxious person, always had been. Drugs and alcohol had helped — way too much, in fact. Now I was both deprived of the opportunity to self-medicate *and* under incredible stress. My anxiety level was barely manageable. I simply couldn't afford to amp my imagined fears with very real ones.

Oddly, I have no recollection of my next bunkie, only that I didn't have to worry about taking my life in my hands climbing down to pee in the middle of the night.

Johann was 65, handsome, and white-haired, a music producer who'd owned a recording studio specializing in solo operatic singers. He'd also put together one of the best classical record collections on the West Coast until legal fees forced him to sell it. We immediately recognized each other as kindred spirits, in a similar state of shock to have discovered that social class and education did not grant us immunity from the consequences of our actions, after all.

Of course, I was dying to know what he'd done, as he fit the profile of an inmate even less than I did. After opening up about my crimes — I always got points for freely admitting guilt in a place where most proclaimed their innocence — I hazarded a guess how he'd landed here.

"Were you entrapped?"

He nodded, incredibly relieved. Finally, he'd met someone here to whom he felt he could unburden himself.

His story began with a friend who'd asked Johann to store a couple of boxes in his garage during a move. Johann knew the magazines featured men "on the young side," but what he didn't know was that his friend had already been arrested for possession of child pornography and was told he could get off with a much lighter sentence ... if he helped snare some other "predators."

Johann had never been with anyone who was close to underage, but admitted he was turned on "by a 16-year-old with a big dick." This was known by Johann's already-in-trouble friend, who invited him down to a big party in LA with promises of a few "young and hung hotties" in attendance. In a taped phone conversation, it was never verbalized that they were specifically minors, a fact that eventually saved Johann from a lengthy sentence. But his mere appearance at the party was enough to get charges filed.

Johann fought it in court for more than two years. But since he possessed the porn in his garage, he was eventually forced to plea bargain. (As I found out over and over again, D.A.'s care about high conviction rates far more than actual guilt or innocence. A guilty plea is a guilty plea — and "busting up a child porn ring" is voter gold when running for higher office.)

I certainly would never defend the sexual exploitation of minors, but Johann's prosecution clearly was a perfect example of the misuse of state resources. His lovers had always been close to his own age, and had he received probation, he never would have been found lurking around playgrounds.

Johann might have been shading the truth, I guess, but in jail the smart man learns not to judge, and I found him both funny and kind. We were basically like a pair of Dorothy Gales, trying to survive the tornados upending our lives (the ones we admittedly walked right into). And we both had Auntie Ems — elderly mothers who were bending as far as they could without breaking. They were both unconditionally forgiving, and for that we had endless gratitude.

We took a perverse solace in the similar fate of Martha Stewart, who was going through her incarceration at exactly the same time we were. I had always been adept at constructing poems and limericks . To amuse Johann, I spun this one:

Martha Stewart's Living—in Jail
We're stunned by the oppression
Impressed by your resolve
(But I'd watch the aggression
when talking to the judge)
Down with the injustice!
Up with Feng Shui'd cells!
(Remember we discussed this —
You'll have to wash with Prell)
Call Leona Helmsley,
She must have some advice
"Buy some shares of Nestle,
The coffee will be nice."
And when the dyke behind you
s'about to lift your dress,
Just say — "May I remind you,
That's been done by CBS."

Avocados

Some of the deputies hated that our dorm possessed the only big-screen TV in the entire jail, but somehow the owner of the Silver Lake disco who had donated it — coincidentally, a man I'd worked next to when we both tended bar in the early '90s — had secured a guarantee that they wouldn't pull it off the wall and hand it to the boys in a regular dorm. However, as a form of group punishment, the cops did take away the extension to the plug for days at a time.

Another political concession to the gay community was the weekly distribution of condoms. Each Wednesday, a butch young lesbian would be shown in by reluctant guards and deliver a short, defiant statement about the right to and necessity of safe sex before she proceeded to hand out Trojans to whoever wanted one. My choice to take one was strictly aspirational, as my libido had set sail for the moment and would not be sighted again in quite some time.

That didn't mean a condom didn't come in handy. One weekend when our viewing privileges had been taken from us, I blew one up and made a balloon. Soon a bunch of us were playing indoor volleyball in the area where we normally watched TV, laughing and carrying on as if we had turned the tube off ourselves because this was so much more fun.

Very few of the deputies seemed to like working at the jail much more than we liked being inmates there, but it was an increasingly rare union job that could support a family and came with a pension. The younger deputies were putting in their requisite time en route to becoming motorcycle cops — the glamorous job they'd joined up for in the first place. Among those guards, we steered clear of a certain type — the ones who'd made it out and blown it, usually because of bad tempers that caused minor traffic stops to escalate into lawsuits. They'd liked riding around town in their shiny boots and aviator glasses, and were furious that threatening a studio exec with their nightstick had gotten them demoted to a windowless dungeon full of L.A.'s flotsam and jetsam.

Unfortunately for us, it was a lot easier to get away with being an angry asshole inside Twin Towers than it was on the wide boulevards of the city. Most of them knew they'd never make work "up top" again, and that just pissed them off even more.

We only rarely saw "gen-pop" prisoners (the straight prisoners in general population) but a line of them would occasionally pass a line of us in the hallway, each group silent, hands behind our backs. We might be going to and from the mess hall, to the library, or back from weekly exercise on the roof.

Once our lines were stopped just as we were perpendicular to each other. We were probably waiting for some kind of "all clear" because a fight had broken out somewhere in the prison, and calm hadn't yet been restored.

The two deputies leading each line engaged in some languid, water-cooler banter as they waited. Then someone from their line raised his hand and the deputy asked what the problem was.

"Abogado. Yo quiero ver un abogado." There was a look on his face of real despair, as if he'd been languishing anonymously for weeks until, finally, another Spanish-speaking inmate had told him he had some rights here, that this wasn't Mexico or Guatemala or Honduras.

"Avocado? You want some avocado?" The deputy's response was in a tone just shy of overt sarcasm, intentionally designed to frustrate the questioner into wondering if he was being mocked or had sincerely been misunderstood.

"Abogado. Yo quiero ver un abogado," repeated the inmate, no doubt suspecting as he heard the words come out of his mouth

that his efforts were in vain.

This guard may not have spoken Spanish, but no one in L.A. can drive three blocks without seeing huge ads on the back of every bus trumpeting *abogados* who will fight like pitbulls for your *derechos* in court, so I wasn't buying it.

Then the other deputy decided to join in the fun.

"I want an avocado too, but I don't think my wife packed one in my lunch today."

His buddy snickered. Humiliated, the inmate gave up. Evidently, he was going to have to wait for a C.O. named Vasquez or Pacheco, and even then have to rely on luck.

I silently fumed at the deputy's contemptuous disregard for someone who could be, for all he knew, completely innocent. I squinted to see the officer's name as I walked past, but got a "Head down, inmate!" barked at me for my trouble.

The perverse thing about law enforcement is how often you hear over and over again, "I love being a cop," or "This is all I ever wanted to do." And yet what I mostly saw were people who didn't seem to like their jobs at all. They might have gotten off on the petty powers they wielded — but that makes for such an ersatz satisfaction.

A few weeks later, one of the "avocado" cops was actually on duty outside of the nurse's office as Jojo and I waited to be called in for a blood draw. (Whether it was Deputy Fric or Deputy Frac I can't say, just that it was one of the two.) Jojo had been telling me about the drama that had landed him in jail, and the way he pronounced a particular word that kept coming up in his story popped a pun into my head. By the time Jojo caught a breath, it had become a punchline, but I hesitated trying it out. Not without a caveat first.

"Hey, Jojo, can I ask you something?"

"Of course, Mark," he answered a little too quickly, perhaps hopeful I was finally going to gauge how he felt about bringing my hairy chest down for a visit to his bottom bunk after lights-out.

"I need to know if this joke in my head can be told by a white person without sounding racist. 'Cause I think it's kind of funny."

"Don't worry, baby, I'll be honest with you."

So I told him, and he laughed. He laughed hard.

"Oh, honey, no, you can't tell that joke. I mean you can, but you can't."

Then he added gleefully, "But I can!"

His laughter had already drawn the attention of the deputy, in a distracted sort of way. Jojo, an entertainer to his core, took immediate advantage.

"You wanna hear a joke, boss?" The C.O. shrugged, feigning indifference, so Jojo spiced the pot.

"It's about cops."

This did evince a slightly perceptible raised eyebrow from the deputy, suddenly curious. Was this black inmate going to diss him to his face?

"Sure."

Jojo winked at me and dove in.

"So, why do you guys deserve a raise?"

The cop eyed him suspiciously, afraid it was a trick question. But he couldn't back out now.

"I'm game. Why?"

With expert timing, Jojo paused, only long enough for the guard to cock his ear. Then he brought it home.

" 'Cause you ain't the *rich*-lice. You da *po*'lice!"

The cop's smile was thoroughly slow and completely reluctant, but he was unable to suppress it. Here was a joke with a little bit of edge but not really mean-spirited, right? He could tell it in the station locker room. And he could preface it quite truthfully with the qualifier that a black inmate had told it to him.

Yet I suspected that somehow after telling the joke with much success to white officers, he would get cocky, and then share it with some black officers. Even if they laughed, he would know it didn't quite sound right when he told it. Suddenly he would be one of the guys the black officers exchanged silent glances about. *That* guy.

The nurse called Jojo in, and I just sat on my little bench, feeling an odd elation, as if I'd just seen the cop sprinkle laxative on his own guacamole.

Rituals

The food was dreadful at L.A. County Jail, and you had to shove it down in 15 minutes. Luckily, the prisoners with HIV were given supplemental rations — basically an extra paper bag lunch daily. When my first canteen came through, I realized how relatively wealthy I was. Some of the other inmates never had a dime put on their books, got no visitors, received no mail. There was a pair of them who latched on to each other because they'd once done time together — the closest thing that passed for a friendship for either of them. Like stray dogs begging for scraps, they would try to cozy up with the most prosperous among us. Easy mark that I was, soon I was sharing my extra PB&J on a nightly basis. Ironically, counseling against such largesse was the first lesson in prison etiquette they taught me in exchange.

"Don't be too generous, Dawg! Dudes will take advantage of you!" commanded Scraggly Blond.

"Er ... but not us," added Skin and Bones hastily, having a firmer grasp of the notion of irony. "We're cool. You can share with guys that are cool."

I learned a lot of dos and don'ts from this funny little duo. Some of their tips ended up proving very valuable.

Drug addicts almost to a man, very few of the inmates even considered using their enforced abstinence as a chance to change the future course, of their life. It was like prison sobriety didn't count because you had no other choice. Nicotine was the drug most of us missed the most, in fact, and I wasted three ramens once to share a pitiful smattering of tobacco in some rolling paper, probably reconstituted from a guard's ground-out butt. (A decade later, I still suffer a sting of regret over that expenditure.

Three soups!)

Most of us hadn't bothered with caffeine in a long time — a hit of the pipe is what got us out of bed. There wasn't even coffee with breakfast, anyway. But the C.O.'s had some, of course, and one of the enterprising kitchen workers managed to smuggle out some ground coffee one day.

We heated water on the sly with one of those plug-in devices that were technically contraband but never got confiscated. The guards pretended not to see. How were we supposed to make the soups the County profited from at the canteen, otherwise? (The showers barely got lukewarm, much less steamy.) But finding a filter was a problem. It turned out that I somehow had an extra pair of clean underwear, and in exchange for the use of it, I got to have two of the cups of the coffee we strained through it.

Having been off of meth for well over a month, the caffeine buzz was about the strongest I've ever felt before or since. Up all night, I watched the pacers — those inmates who, like Jeff, walked the perimeter of the dorm most of the night, some no doubt high on something else besides coffee. Scraggly Blond told me who one of these perennial walkers was.

"He's head of the 18th Street Gang."

This didn't mean much to me. Gang-wise, I only knew of the Crips and the Bloods, and he definitely wasn't either of those. In fact, he looked Italian.

Scraggly Blond was agog.

"You've never heard of the 18th Street Gang? Are you serious?"

Obviously I hadn't been around the block nearly as much as I thought I had.

"He sure doesn't look gay to me," I noted stupidly.

"Of course, he's not gay! He uses the gay dorms like... protective custody."

Better to get whispered about than shanked by the colleague of someone you had murdered, I guess.

I would have anticipated fights breaking out over what to watch on TV; instead, within jail reigned the most smoothly functioning democracy I'd ever seen. If there was any disagreement, someone would call out "vote!" and the issue would be settled in an instant.

Occasionally, a group of inmates rounded up votes ahead of time, just to make sure they'd see a certain show. One such night was the pilot of *America's Top Model*, during which Tyra Banks was going to introduce her first single, "Shake Ya Body," in a glossy music video. Evidently, she was the obsession of a funny little Latina queen, Cindy, who corralled support for the viewing days in advance.

The night of the show, Cindy dressed up. Deprived of any appropriate raw material, she went for simple elegance — a well-draped bed sheet over her bare-shouldered body. Rapt and still as an Athenian statue, Cindy shushed anyone who dared talk during the show.

Ms. Navarro was a middle-aged Latina guard who reminded me of one of those junior high school teachers who would insist yours was the absolute worst class she'd ever taught. Although I think she was more amused than anything else, she felt obliged to command Cindy to get back into her uniform. Cindy waved back her acknowledgment, but just dipped behind some bunks during the commercials. As the hour wore on and Ms. Navarro repeated her order, we started to wonder if Cindy was going to end up in trouble for her insubordination.

Finally, the music video came on. Cindy, who had heretofore maintained the poise of a beauty pageant contestant, burst into a mad choreography — part '60s go-go girl, part whirling dervish. Somehow, she managed to keep her eyes gyroscopically fixed on the screen the entire time. When the video finished, she turned to face us, and the entire dorm burst into thunderous applause.

Ms. Navarro, on the other hand, was getting seriously impatient.

"Get back into your uniform, inmate! That sheet is county property, not a dress, and you are about to get yourself thrown in the tank!"

Cindy scurried back to her bunk and reappeared toga-less soon enough, reduced once again to the regulation orange pants (with an oh-so-fashionable elastic waistband) and a white-t-shirt. She said she was sorry, but she clearly wasn't. And who could blame her? We'd almost certainly given her the only standing ovation she'd *ever* receive.

The general air of insubordination that Tyra and Cindy induced probably had something to do with what occurred the next day, an event that prompted me to write the first short story of my incarceration, Ink.

Ink

It's an early March evening in the Los Angeles County Men's Central Jail, Section K-11, Dorm 5100. I can't be sure of the exact time because, as in a casino, there are no clocks or windows here by which to measure the progress of the day. It's extremely disorienting at first, but then you get used to it. Perhaps it's even a good thing. Maybe time goes by a little faster when you're not quite sure of its pace.

K-11 is where they put all the gay inmates — at least those savvy enough to check the right box during intake. Since the mid-'90s, when crystal meth exploded in the gay community, a lot of guys no one ever thought would end up in jail did just that. These were men with private attorneys hired by horrified families, lawyers who could make a serious dent in a Corrections budget with just one wrongful death lawsuit. It was a no-brainer for the Sheriff's Department to institute the gay dorms.

And you've never seen so many grateful converts to the virtues of segregation on the basis of sexual orientation than the inmates themselves. Jail is bad enough without having to go back in the closet just to survive it.

I'm lying on my bunk while reading a trashy, dog-eared bestseller. Suddenly, "On your bunks!" is barked over the intercom.

We're used to this order on a daily basis, but it's always followed by "Count time!" But it's a good hour before Count. Something's not right.

Instinctively, I locate my one piece of contraband, a black ink PaperMate pen purchased at the steep price of three Ramen soups and two candy bars from the occupant of the bunk to my right, Jack Hammer. That's not the name on his birth certificate, of course, but most everyone here has a nickname, and Jack's got one of the best.

I slip the pen into a Colgate carton and stretch out on my stomach as the door to the dorm swings open. "Radio!" is called out, followed by "Walking!" ("Radio" is prison slang for "Quiet," and "Walking" means guards have entered the room.)

The deputies converge somewhat alarmingly in my direction, but they head straight for Jack's bunk. My neighbor is not just a purveyor of contraband pens, but the dorm dealer of Wellbutrin, an antidepressant that is ground up and snorted here for the cheapest of highs. Compared with heroin or crystal meth, the buzz is a bit of a joke, but the ritual of copping and using together remains a powerful draw for addicts (which means virtually everyone here). Jack is also the tattoo-artist-in-residence, and practicing his craft requires a battery-powered device that is strictly prohibited. Or maybe not so strictly, considering somebody had to smuggle in the batteries, maybe even one of the very deputies tossing his bunk.

Too bad they're not searching for irony. It's everywhere here.

Heavily inked himself, Jack has a tattoo of an eagle with wings spread across the back of his head, a swastika serving as its beating heart. You'd think the insignia of the Aryan Brotherhood would be a problem with the black inmates, but Jack gets along with them just fine.

It didn't take me long to realize that the gay dorms have evolved into a refuge for an entire subset of straight men who find the politics of gangbanging in gen-pop exhausting. Once a few of them discovered it was a safer place to await trial, enough of them did it so that time here is now not necessarily considered proof of a sexual orientation that could be lethal to one's reputation back on the street.

Besides, the gay dorms are the best place for a heterosexual man in prison to get laid.

This is where the girls are after all, specifically the "trannies"

— a catch-all term running the gamut from drag queen to pre-op transgender. Some couldn't pass for female on the outside, nor would even try. In here, they're employing a survival strategy. Others — street prostitutes who specialize in a certain clientele — have already had their top half done and sport a rather impressive rack. They seem the least interested in having a prison boyfriend, perhaps because sex has been a transaction to them for far too long. No one's story is simple in here.

Let's just say that a "he" who goes by "she" will do a pretty good job of exuding feminine energy. For the straight inmate who spends more time in jail than out, K-11 is where he'll get his most realistic shot at romance.

Jack's "girlfriend" in here is Kay. Considering his square-jawed skinhead swagger, Kay is a surprising choice for a partner. It's clear that she's not had any hormone therapy, and the Mary-Ann-on-Gilligan's-Island knotting of her t-shirt beneath her diaphragm does little to bolster the illusion of breasts. And neither her wetted-pencil eyeliner nor small rubber-banded bun compensate for her distinct Adam's apple and Eileen Heckart rasp.

Simply put, Kay is a plain Jane. But she seems to understand that in cases like hers the best defense is a good offense. She fawns over Jack like a well-trained geisha and Jack returns the affection unabashedly. Kay is probably pretty good in the sack as well, or at least skilled at distracting from the obvious. In the shower, I hear Jack tell a friend, "Hell, I've been hooked up with Kay for a year and a half now, and I still haven't seen her dick!"

If true love is blind, then prison love is at least glaucoma.

Unfortunately for the happy couple, Kay does not sleep here. She is assigned to one of the other two gay dorms on the floor, 5200. Where Jack and I are, 5100, is to 5200 as a gated community is to a trailer park. As for the third dorm, 5300, it's where you get sent for fighting, for talking back to a guard, for stealing. I've seen the denizens of 5300 in line for chow, and it is eminently clear why their dorm is known as "Thunderdome."

After meals, sometimes the residents of 5100 and 5200, whose entryways are opposite each other, engage in "roaming," i.e., visiting friends in the other dorm. This is allowed by some, but not all, of the guards who work in the booth overlooking both dorms. It's during these tolerated intermezzos that Kay slips in for a quick tête-à-tête with Jack.

Or used to. Three days ago, Kay was sent to the Hole, for what offense I do not know. Somehow I think she knew she was going, though. Her last roaming visit to Jack was noticeably tender, even intimate, one of those private moments you accidentally witness and only realize in retrospect was a farewell.

The next afternoon, I watched Jack receive a note smuggled out from Kay. I tried to make out what it said, reading upside-down, but quickly averted my eyes when Jack looked up. That's the kind of nosiness that gets you in trouble in prison, and the only thing worse than being transferred to Thunderdome would be getting a beat-down from Jack Hammer.

Now, three days after Kay's disappearance, as Jack's bunk is tossed, the deputies snarl and puff like a pride of lions during a kill. They immediately find his stash of PaperMates and Wellbies, which they empty, along with his considerable store of canteen food, into a large Hefty trash bag. In an empty bunk next to Jack's, they find his tattooing device — or perhaps pretend to, as they might just be putting on a show to maintain the illusion that an informant hadn't already told them exactly where it was.

I lie quietly like a baby impala quivering in the savanna, thinking only of my precious pen. As I watch Jack being handcuffed and led away to the Hole, I feel bad for him. Even more, I feel relief for myself.

I am a writer, and writing is what is getting me through this experience. The nubby, eraserless golf pencils they give us might as well be gray crayons. My pen is like gold to me.

Like Jack ... I ink; therefore I am.

After the guards have departed with their prey, the vultures

— me included — swoop down to scavenge what's left. Our stated intention is to hold onto everything that's been unconfiscated in order to return it to Jack when he emerges from solitary.

(In my case, this is actually true. 30 days later, I will hand him back, with genuine gratitude, his copy of Larry McMurtry's *The Evening Star*, a book I enjoyed immensely during his absence.)

When things calm down, the buzz after Jack's abrupt departure is about whether someone (or who?) dropped a dime on him. Whispers circulate like bees in a meadow, but no one is stung with an accusation.

They do not know what I know. I saw the look on Jack's face when he read Kay's note. I saw him hold back tears — not something an Aryan Brother should be seen shedding over a chick-with-a-dick. He's supposed to be thinking of the "real" girl waiting for him on the outside, the one who will smuggle things to him on visiting day in her real vagina. But Jack doesn't love that girl, genuine (and useful) genitalia notwithstanding. Jack loves Kay.

My instinctive conclusion, the one I share with no one, is that Jack informed on himself.

It was the only means he could devise to get close to Kay. He might have even been able to arrange to get the cell next to her, or perhaps the same schedule for the shower. At the very least, he will be able to send her "kites" far more easily, you only need to promise a corridor-cleaning porter a few packets of instant soup to make that happen.

I do hope that someone manages to smuggle Jack a pen. Kay will want to read his notes over and over, and if the words are written in pencil, they may fade.

Mrs. Kendal

You'd think that a nominally heterosexual man like Jack Hammer would have sought a relationship among the more classically transgendered girls in the dorm — by which I mean the inmates who'd had breast implants and lived as females on the outside. They still had male genitalia, which is why they were put in the men's dorms.

But Jack fell into a neither-here-nor-there category for which current terminology falls short; he wasn't gay, but he wasn't really straight either. He clearly liked overlapping genders, but seemed to be more attracted to a man who "played" a woman than to a biological man who could actually pass for a woman. Jack would have given Alfred Kinsey a migraine.

Among the cohort of breast-sporting trans girls, it was hard not to notice Sylvia in particular; although I suppose being noticed had been the whole point of her getting implants that big in the first place. Oddly enough, what no doubt made her a lot of money outside jail seemed to embarrass her in here; her self-consciousness at all the wide-eyed looks was palpable. It was impossible to pretend you didn't see them.

Every morning, a few inmates at a time were roused early because they had a court date, and Sylvia's and mine fell on the same day. On the bus downtown we were separated from the straight prisoners, but not from their catcalling. By dint of sheer proximity to Sylvia, I learned how vulnerable it feels to be the object of so much unwanted attention. I felt sorry for her. After a deputy banged his nightstick enough to quiet the rowdies, Sylvia and I got to talking. Like strangers on a train, except in handcuffs.

Originally, Sylvia came from Guatemala to sew jeans in an

East L.A. sweatshop, but soon discovered she could make *much* better money as a prostitute. Other job perks included performing in drag, a little cocaine, and eventually, a sugar daddy who paid for her breasts.

From what I could gather — we spoke in a hodgepodge of English and Spanish — she was in jail because she'd taken the fall for something he'd done. I didn't push for details, mindful of Larry's warning not to be too nosy, "In here, the only thing worse than talking too much is listening too much."

One of the few benefits of being stuck for hours in a courtroom basement was that it gave you access to a phone. You could make all the local calls you wanted, provided you could remember the phone numbers you'd probably bequeathed long ago to the speed dial of your cell phone.

Sylvia made one very lengthy call. At first she was comforting, repeating over and over that she, too, wished she were with him. Then she asked if he'd been drinking. After that, weariness crept into her voice, tinged with impatience. I had the distinct impression that she felt just as trapped by her life outside of jail as her life inside of it.

On the return bus ride, we drove down Melrose, which at one point placed us only two blocks away from my apartment. I fantasized about the driver magically letting me out, all of this a forgotten nightmare. But I also knew I probably needed to go through everything I was about to go through, however unpleasant.

I also realized that passersby were going out of their way to avoid looking up at us. It felt awfully lonely to be invisible, but I couldn't really blame them. They just wanted the bus with the grated windows to move along so they didn't have to contend with thinking about the human beings inside. When it came to the incarcerated, out of sight was truly out of mind.

That afternoon I had pled guilty to several counts — possession with intent to sell, fraud, and forgery. My actual sentence would come down in another month or so, depending on the deal my lawyer could get me. But I would definitely be going to prison.

Psychologically, I stood at the entrance to a long dark cave, knowing I had no choice but to walk through it. I felt both afraid and strangely relieved. I would finally be suffering the consequences of my actions.

I was so tired of getting away with things.

Back at the jail, everyone who had been to court that day was put in a holding tank, and we were escorted, two by two, back to our respective dorms. Sylvia and I were the last two left. As we waited for the guard to come get us, a porter swept up debris that lay in front of the cells.

I spotted an empty plastic Coca-Cola bottle and asked him if he could give it to us. It was a small luxury, but it would mean I didn't have to trek to the bathroom in 5100 to drink from the faucet every time I was thirsty. The porter picked it up but did not hand it over. Instead, he held it slightly away. He wanted something in return.

I had actually managed to take a *National Geographic* with me to read during the hours in the courthouse anteroom. Is that what he wanted? Perhaps the porters at Los Angeles Men's County Jail had an unsuspected interest in "The Lost Tribes of Peruvian Amazon."

I pointed to the magazine, just to make sure, but he rolled his eyes.

"Fuck no, dawg!"

I was at a complete loss. But Sylvia wasn't.

With a resigned shrug, she popped open the snaps of her jumpsuit, flashing her perfectly round silicon breasts for a long two-second count.

And I thought he wanted my *National Geographic.* God, I could be an egghead.

Satisfied, the porter handed the container over, then finished filling his bag of trash. I averted my eyes as Sylvia tucked her breasts back in, suddenly modest.

I had a distinct sense of déjà vu, even though I was quite certain I'd never been in a remotely similar situation. Only later that night, when I lay in my bunk with my full plastic Coke bottle of lousy-tasting water, did I realize what struck me as familiar.

I'd first seen *The Elephant Man* on Broadway 30 years before. The protagonist, John Merrick, makes an unlikely journey from sideshow attraction to fashionable *accoutrement* in the trendiest London salons. Fully aware that his grotesque appearance means he daren't hope for reciprocation, he nonetheless falls in love with a celebrated actress who befriends him, Madge Kendal.

In the play's most moving scene, she provides Merrick with the sole moment of his entire life that will approach sexual intimacy.

Mrs. Kendal shows him her naked breasts.

Somehow this realization made it impossible to sleep. Johann was the only person there who might appreciate the anecdote, but it was past lights out. The only thing to do was get it out of my head and down on paper.

Ironically, the showers were the only place with enough light to write. If I got thirsty, I wouldn't need my water bottle to save me a trip after all.

Black Widow

I was sentenced to 16 months, which meant I would serve eight, before being eligible for parole. (This is "half-time," and standard procedure unless otherwise specified by a judge.) About four weeks after my sentencing, I was told that I would be transferred early the next morning, or "catching the chain" in prison slang. I would first go to Delano, one of the reception centers where inmates basically wait eight weeks or so for a final assignment. No one has phone privileges there, so I made what would be my last calls for a couple of months.

In line to make a call, I found myself next to Wynn, whom I knew as a fellow aficionado of the *L.A. Times* daily crossword puzzle. He had one of those faces that a modicum of charm would have rendered quite beautiful, but unfortunately he tended to confuse wit with sarcasm. He was aggressively skeptical at my news.

"*No one* gets sent upstate that soon after sentencing, honey. No one."

A month didn't seem particularly speedy to me, but to Wynn, it was the very definition of alacrity. He'd been at County for the better part of a year, trying to beat a charge of negligent homicide in the drug overdose of his older boyfriend. I'd found this out, oddly enough, when the clue for 22-Across was "post-coital arachnid."

"Black widow," Wynn had muttered. "Just like me."

There in line for the phone, Wynn told me he'd just found out that the D.A. had made him a final offer. If Wynn didn't take it, his case would go to trial. Empty threats, insisted Wynn. One call to his wealthy mother in Indiana would clear up this misunderstanding, pronto.

According to Wynn, the lawyer was *obviously* incompetent. A guilty plea? Absurd! Wynn would accept nothing less than a full exoneration. Hell, he would *countersue*! By the time he placed the call, Wynn was spending the imagined settlement money on a house in the Hollywood Hills.

Even hearing just one side of the conversation, it wasn't hard to figure out that this wasn't the first time Wynn had asked his mother to fire a lawyer. It seemed, however, this was the first time she'd refused.

Wynn whined, wheedled, and whimpered, but his mother had finally found her spine. Involuntary manslaughter was the offer, take it or leave it. With luck, she added unconvincingly, he might even get time served.

Wynn's crocodile tears dried the moment he hung up. *It could have been worse*, I thought he'd say, as he handed me the receiver. *It could have been murder.*

No such gratitude was forthcoming. Which is not to say he couldn't muster his own verdict for the woman who'd clearly written her last check on his behalf.

"*Such a bitch.*"

At three in the morning, I was roused and told to gather the few things I was allowed to take along. These were a manila envelope holding the letters that had been written to me, and a paperback whose title I can't recall. Unfortunately, there wasn't enough light to read, and I just sat in the semi-darkness, trying to enjoy the rare stillness of relative quiet.

Larry sat next to me, even though I had said my goodbyes the night before.

"I forgot to give you something."

For a moment I thought he'd get uncharacteristically sentimental and give me a hug. But instead he handed me some toilet paper.

"I had to learn that lesson the hard way."

There were only a few of us inside the holding tank, and after I gingerly stepped over someone sleeping in the dead center of the floor, I was grateful to find the last free corner. With a little luck, I thought, perhaps I could doze off, too. (The toilet paper Larry had given me somehow felt like a security blanket.)

I had just drifted off when the moaning started. I tried to ignore it, but it went beyond some fitful soundtrack to a bad dream. A fellow I hadn't even noticed before was on the floor of the tank, writhing in discomfort.

He started pleading to see a guard, claiming to have had a heart attack the week before, and in dire need of returning to the hospital. I surmised he was most probably suffering from heroin withdrawal, but that hardly made it less unpleasant. Dope sick is on par with food poisoning when it comes to feeling like you are about to die.

After what seemed like a solid hour, I started to press the "emergency" intercom. Finally, after 20 minutes or so, a deputy answered and asked what was wrong.

I resisted an overwhelming urge to mention how many times I'd rung the buzzer, and stuck to the point at hand.

"There's a guy here who's really sick. *Seriously.*"

There was a sigh, then silence. I felt the wary eyes of the other men in the cell on me, as if they were afraid my do-gooding would somehow get them all in trouble.

The intercom crackled back on.

"He's seriously sick?"

'No,' I thought sarcastically, 'I'm just bored and felt like playing with the buzzer.'

"Yes, I think he's seriously sick."

Unexpectedly, I got some support from the peanut gallery.

"Yeah, man, we don't want him dying in here."

A big burly black guy had piped up from the corner. Smart. Appeal to their fear of a wrongful death lawsuit.

It worked. A few minutes later, a deputy appeared. He leaned over the sick prisoner and gathered just enough information for the paperwork he would have to fill out later.

"So what's going on?"

"Man, I was in the hospital last week... I had a heart attack... I need to go back..."

He clutched at his chest and gasped for air. If he was acting, he deserved an Oscar.

The C.O. gave a go-ahead on his walkie-talkie, and a minute or so later some medics appeared with a stretcher.

I made sure to thank the officer, who asked me if I knew the guy. I shook my head. That was enough small talk for both of us.

There in the cavernous, windowless basement of the County Jail, the daytime fluorescents turned on. It was the closest we ever got to sunrise.

Jerome Punjab Freeze

The cell I shared for the first two weeks at Delano was right out of the movies — cramped and dank, a walk-in closet — an apt metaphor if there ever was one.

There were no gay dorms on the "mainline." The last time I'd had to "pass" was working on Wall Street 20 years ago, just before I'd moved to California. If it had seemed like the politic thing to do back then, now it felt like a matter of life and death.

The first time the door to the cell closed behind me, I reminded myself for the umpteenth time what Scraggly Blond had told me.

"A two-man cell is pretty safe, because if your cellie hurts you, he pretty much knows he's going to be the only suspect. That's some serious extra time on his term. Generally speaking, he's not going to risk it."

Generally speaking.

But I got lucky. In fact, it's hard to imagine how I could have gotten any luckier than I was by getting Mack as a cellmate. He was age 32 or so, funny and gentle, and I had no trouble believing he bore no resemblance to the blackout drunk who'd impulsively committed armed robbery a year before. (When the police finally tracked him down, he'd just celebrated six months' sobriety. "That's nice," said the judge, "Congratulations. And perhaps that *was* your finger under your jacket instead of a gun. But the cashier didn't know that, and she's still having nightmares. Eight years.")

Besides Alcoholics Anonymous, Mack loved two things — cooking and writing fantasy fiction. A.A. and making food were not immediate options, but his last vocation made us a perfect match. We had no books, but we had pencil and paper and imaginations that honored no walls. We were writing stories for each other by the third day.

I proposed a daily exercise using a premise I'd picked up from watching improv troupes take suggestions from the audience.

"Give me a name, a place, and an event," was the prompt. I don't remember the ones I supplied Mack, but still have what I wrote based on the ones he supplied me.

Curly. Albuquerque. The Holocaust.
Leroy Jefferson. A nursing home. Glendale.
Jerome Punjab Freeze. The Australian outback. A barbecue.

That one took me aback. "'Jerome Punjab Freeze?' Where the hell did you come up with that?"

Mack smiled innocently, but I soon discovered he'd been an aficionado of *Dungeons and Dragons* for years and had a long history of coming up with outlandish names.

I would sit at the tiny table that served as a desk and he would sit on the top bunk. In the course, of an afternoon, we'd each devise a short story covering the three elements we had listed for each other.

I got a handle on "Jerome Punjab Freeze" by imagining him to be a polyglot Aussie returning to his odd little town in the hinterlands, negotiating the bizarre politics of his extended half-immigrant/half-aboriginal family. It wasn't half-bad.

Mack was a natural storyteller, if not a literary one. No matter. We were entranced by each other's stories; the "ultimate captive audience," I joked. We formed our own secret society in that tiny cell, listening to each other with all the attentiveness of a lover making sure his partner reaches orgasm. In a space of suffocating physical intimacy, we found a psychological intimacy that temporarily (and temporally) liberated us.

Mack and I were both called out the same morning, me to D-Block, he to C-Block. While relieved that we were leaving that cramped space, we both felt the tension and fear that accompanies any change of circumstances in prison. We were pretty sure we'd see each other on the yard in the next six weeks, but just in case, I gave him my sister's address so that he could write to me through her.

Our new dorms were on different schedules and so we never did see each other trudging around the track. But I knew he was as grateful as I was to be in the sun again, even for a little while.

I did make a new friend that first day during Yard, and our encounter prompted a memory that I turned into my second short story. It was the first of many I wrote for my mother to keep reassuring her that nothing she had done (or *not* done) had led to my unfortunate present circumstance.

Pistachios

I first encountered the footwear known as espadrilles in August 1969. I was almost 11 years old, the fourth of five children, and my mother had decided to take all five of us back to her native France for the summer.

Camping out on a farm beside a lake that was just outside of a village named Salles-Curan, we joined my aunt Francoise and her four children, along with Francoise's pregnant best friend, Paulette Polignac, and her brood of eight. (My dad stayed behind in New York, and the two French husbands came up for a few weekends.)

Later, even my mother wondered if she was a bit touched in the head for traveling alone with five young children, but she'd actually done it before with us in 1962, when we were mostly preschoolers. At airports and train stations, strangers would regularly marvel at how well behaved we were. My mother's formula was brilliantly simple and thoroughly French. She showered us with affection, and then disciplined us with the mere threat of withdrawing that affection. Simply put, she was far more likely to raise an eyebrow than her voice.

The Perdriolles (my cousins) and the Polignacs (their friends) were raised in the same vein; but collectively, the 17 of us kids constituted a small mob. With all those mouths to feed three times a day, my aunt had sensibly arranged for use of the farmer's kitchen for the main meals. Because it usually accommodated the feeding of the farmhands, the dining room was as big as the mess hall at a typical American sleep-away camp — at least that's how I remember it. It had to have been big to fit us all, especially when Paulette's brood, who mostly just ate at their tents, joined the rest of us for special occasions or when it rained.

That summer represented my mother's fondest hope that her five children would get lost in the *sauce blanche* of my cousins and their Kennedyesque friends, and we would return to the States as the bilingual family she'd always dreamed we'd be. Equally divided between girls and boys, the Polignacs were tan, athletic, and just the right amount of rambunctious. We Olmsted kids were perfectly adequate and sociable on our home turf, but in France we came off as insular and tongue-tied. Despite my mother's valiant efforts, we knew little more French than the words of a memorized nursery rhyme about a mouse dipped in oil.

Her grand plan had been waylaid years before when my brother Steve, the eldest, had struggled to absorb English on top of the French and Spanish he already spoke. (My parents had lived in France and Chile in the mid-'50s before coming to the U.S.) But when he felt lost in a New Jersey elementary school, a well-meaning second-grade teacher suggested that my parents switch to English for a while.

Within a few months, Steve's trilingualism was so derailed that he blocked his ears when he heard any language not spoken by his American friends. Later, my mother ruefully recounted how he came back from school the following year eager to show her that he'd learned to count to ten in Spanish. In her flawless but French-accented English, she would imitate his chewy American pronunciation, "ooo-noh, doe-is, tray-ss..." one accent on top of another on top of another.

She still had hopes for the rest of us, though, and that summer was to jumpstart the process. She did her best to separate us from each other early in the summer, and my solo immersive experience had been with the Louveteaux — the French Cub Scouts. Our camp was on a small mountain overlooking a sweet little village by the name of Nant, and when word spread that there was "un garçon Americain" in the troop, it gained us admittance to the priest's house on the day of the moon landing so we could witness this historic event on TV. Ironically, I was indistinguishable from the other 20 or so jeunes garçons in berets sitting cross-legged in front of the set, except for the frustrated look on my face as I tried to puzzle out what Neil Armstrong was saying under the damned interpreter's instantaneous French translation. One big step for whom? Anne Kind? Who was Anne Kind?

I might have learned more French had there not been a bilingual half-English boy there, Bernard, who was often dragooned to translate for me. Given my provenance, I was expected to know a thing or two about Cowboys and Indians, but I preferred playing French Resistance vs. the Gestapo. It seemed we were each fascinated by the historical mythos of the other. Truthfully, I didn't really mind what we played, as long as I was captured and tied up. I'm sure it was the fantasy of a few other boys, but I only realized years later that bondage is a fetish so ubiquitous it is practically banal.

The notion that a gay child might experience sexual stirrings is much more accepted now, even if it still tends to be couched in vague terms along the lines of, "I always knew I was different." Yes, I knew I was "different." I also knew there were some boys I wanted to look at more than others, and one of them was Jean-Pierre Polignac.

He was a year older than I, on the cusp of puberty, and already handsome in an adult way. He was the best soccer player in the troop and flashed the smile of an undeniable winner every time he scored a goal. I knew the other boys also looked up to him, but I didn't think most of them cared whether he played le foot with his shirt off.

I had an excuse to hang around Jean-Pierre a lot at camp because he was the best friend of my cousin, Emmanuel. The obligation to be a helpful relative irritated Manu, who alternated between including me and trying to ditch me. Jean-Pierre maintained a breezy graciousness either way, but by the time we got to

Salles-Curan, where all three families joined each other, Manu seemed to act as the gatekeeper to all of the Polignacs.

I was oddly relieved, already painfully aware that my attraction to Jean-Pierre was part of something far more profound unfolding inside me. I often went off on my own, even cultivating a friendship of sorts with one of the farmhands, who let me drive around with him on the tractor, and after repeated pleas, gave me my first cigarette. He wasn't particularly attractive, but my eyes kept landing on his sinewy forearms as he turned the tractor wheel. Whether he was merely bemused by my attentions or something else altogether, I can't be sure.

I would often drift into the kitchen to watch the three mothers prepare lunch or dinner. "Watch" isn't the right word, really. I listened. I had a pet theory that if I concentrated hard enough, I would suddenly understand every word. Although they certainly appreciated my desire to learn French, they were no doubt relieved that I had no idea what they were saying. It was their vacation too, after all, and if they were going to spend just as many hours in the kitchen as they did at home, they were at least going to luxuriate in extended conversation with other women. (I may not have known what they were saying, but I did notice that they laughed a lot more with each other than they did with their husbands.)

Usually my mother would tell me to join the other kids playing outside, but sometimes I'd be put to work peeling carrots or snapping off the ends of green beans. I would look around the room, and repeat phrases fed to me by my mother, like, "Je vois la fenêtre" or "la table est grande." One day I wanted to know what those shoes were that I'd seen Jacques the farmhand wearing.

"They're called espadrilles," explained my mom. I made her repeat it several times, but a few minutes later, could not retrieve the word. Instead, I referred to them as "pistachios."

And then I asked her if I could get a pair.

This was truly an odd request, similar to a Long Island kid

visiting Miami and asking for white loafers just like his Great Uncle Sid's. What I couldn't explain was how much they resembled the footwear adorning Jonny Quest, an animated television character on whom I'd had an enormous crush since 1964. Jonny wore white pants and black turtlenecks and got into cool adventures with his sidekick Hadji and dog, Bandit. Jonny's father, Dr. Benton Quest, had a suspiciously well-built best friend, "Race" Bannon. There was not a woman in sight. I wasn't even sure Jonny Quest had a mother, much less hung out in the kitchen with her and her gal-pals when they cooked. (An activity that was also of no interest to Jean-Pierre Polignac, who butchly hightailed it out of there the second he finished his morning café au lait.)

Paulette, Jean-Pierre's mother, often smiled at me while she cooked. I found out later that she had an "interior decorator" brother, and I think she saw in me many of the traits she'd seen in him growing up.

But not understanding any of this at the time, it was a complete surprise to me when she brought up the wish I'd voiced a week before.

"Do you still want some espadrilles, Mark?"

I looked to my own mother to make sure I understood. It hadn't occurred to me that she would mention my whim to anyone else, much less authorize it, and I was completely thrown off. Suddenly I felt the need to be the voice of responsibility.

"But... can we afford them?"

My mother translated, and they both laughed. Yes, she reassured me, we can afford them. (I had no idea they were as almost as cheap as flip-flops.)

My real concern was provoking the resentment of my siblings, of my cousins, of the Polignac clan. No one got a special trip into the village with one of the mothers. Surely, they would find such personal attention exceedingly undemocratic.

Paulette didn't seem to care. I could see where Jean-Paul got that breezy manner of his.

Soon we were rambling into town in the family Citroën, parking right on the cobblestoned sidewalk the way you still could in a French village in 1969. I waited for us to visit the butcher and the baker, but mine seemed to be our only errand. We found one of those catchall shops that sold everything a summer tourist could want, brushing through the hanging beads the French use instead of screen doors to keep out flies.

The salesman was a little flummoxed at our request.

"Espadrilles? Vous êtes sûr?"

By then, I wasn't sûr at all anymore. But I couldn't really back down now.

A few minutes later I had a pair of turquoise espadrilles and a hefty case of buyer's remorse. I could tell they didn't give me the slightest soupçon of Johnny Questdom. What had I been thinking?

I could only smile and use one of the few French words I had down pat.

"Merci, Paulette."

She put her arm around me, but instead of returning to the car, ushered me to a sidewalk café. There she treated me to an Orangina that was probably more expensive than my new footwear. She had a coffee.

My inability to communicate in French was probably my strongest asset just then. Because what Paulette had been after all along was no doubt just to have 15 minutes of what passed in her life as solitude, watching the crowd go by, her thoughts all her own.

Fast-forward to 35 years later. I have recently arrived at North Kern State Prison in Delano, California. It is my first Yard. This basically means 12 or so revolutions walking around a gravel track. A few inmates have sneakers because they've been here long enough to order from the outside. Newbies like me have to make do with prison-issue cloth loafers.

What was the French word for these again? It's on the tip of my tongue, but I can't quite retrieve it. I'm not even sure what they're called in English. Pistachios? All I know is that they keep slipping off; just like the pair I owned decades before.

I notice that another inmate seems to be following me in a fashion, sort of behind me and to the side. But I get no aggressive vibes from him. Rather the opposite.

When our eyes meet, he approaches.

"Hey, dude, what's your name?" he asks, completely friendly. I tell him and return the question.

"I'm Extra," he answers, extending his hand.

Unlike some, he doesn't have to explain his nickname. He is a good 50 pounds overweight.

I don't mind the company, but I am a little suspicious.

"So, those flapjacks are kind of annoying, huh?"

Flapjacks? All I can think that he's talking about are pancakes. Then he points to my feet. Oh.

"Your flapjacks. They don't fit so good."

So that's what they call them in English (or at least "prisonese.") And in that moment the French word comes back to me, but this doesn't seem like the time or place to share this information.

Then Extra points to his own feet.

"See what I did?"

Extra has fashioned holes in his flapjacks, threaded laces through them, and created de facto sneakers that fit him snugly.

"I can do that for you, if you want…"

I realize now why he was shadowing me, but I don't mind. Resourcefulness is an art form in prison. And I am not naïve enough to think he's offering this service out of the goodness of his heart.

"How much?"

"A book of stamps."

I'm not particularly deft yet at the kind of "canteen calcu-

lus" that seems to be second nature to some of these guys, but it strikes me as a little steep.

Extra senses my hesitation and sweetens the pot.

"And I'll throw in a tube of toothpaste too."

I still have no idea if that makes it a good deal, but I vaguely remember that I will be asked to contribute something to the dorm "kitty," and figure I can use the toothpaste for that. (Its contents are distributed to guys coming out of the Hole who return to bunks confiscated of all personal items. Of course, each race has its own, so my tube will go in the white kitty.)

It sounds like a fair exchange. Still, I instinctively hesitate, just so it doesn't seem like I'm an easy mark. So Extra tries a classic sales ploy of trying to make the buyer care about why the seller needs this to happen.

"I don't write a lot of letters or nothin', but the guys who sell tobacco here only take books of stamps. And, man, I have a wicked nicotine addiction."

Delano, being a reception center, has more restrictive rules than whatever prison we will eventually get assigned to for the remainder of our sentences. Tobacco can't be purchased here at the commissary, but of course, it's smuggled in. Extra would have probably elicited more sympathy from me if he told me that he needed the stamps for letters home, but I have been a smoker on and off for years, so I get that too. Plus being quite the letter-writer, I am well-stocked with stamps. I agree to his terms.

Not too much later, in the Day Room, Extra approaches me with his contraband razor and laces, which are thin strips sliced from blue state-issued bed sheets. He cuts small holes in the flapjacks through which he then pushes the laces and draws them tight.

He carries on an amiable monologue while he works, but I am distracted by the way one of his eyes seem to be on his work, while the other seems to be looking at me. I suddenly wonder if his nickname comes from an extra chromosome, but I keep that little joke to myself.

When he's finished, I try them out, walking across the floor in front of him just as I did for Paulette in that little *magasin* all those years ago. A repressed memory suddenly makes its way to the surface. The salesman had said they weren't tight enough in the back and would slip off. But I had mistrusted his advice and insisted to Paulette that they fit fine. Within hours I'd known he was right, and spent the rest of the trip continually slipping them back up on my heels, each time kicking myself for simply not having tried another pair.

Extra's modification makes these flapjacks fit snugly, and I feel strangely redeemed for my contrariness of decades before. I hand him the book of stamps, and he hands me a tube of toothpaste. Later, my bunkie will tell me I was way overcharged, and I will just shrug, like that Salles-Curan salesman who didn't really care if a ten-year-old American boy wanted to buy the wrong size espadrilles.

What I won't tell my bunkie is why the transaction with Extra takes on a sudden meaning that very afternoon, when I open the first piece of mail I receive at Delano. It is a letter from my Aunt Francoise, the third mother in that farm kitchen in 1969. I have remained very close to her over the years, and her unconditional love through this experience has humbled me to the point of tears.

She tells me that the breast cancer which Paulette Polignac had battled years before has aggressively returned, and the family is supporting her decision to forgo any new treatment. My aunt knows that I will want to write her.

And now, instead of groping for platitudes, or awkwardly sharing anything about my present circumstances, I will be able to tell her a funny little story that speaks to the power of a small kindness and has nothing at all to do with pistachios.

PART TWO
DELANO* SYCAMORE*BIRCH*CEDAR

Politics

This new giant dormitory is proving to be sociologically interesting, to say the least. For example — many major announcements, along the lines of "hang out at your bunks like good boys for another five minutes," are issued in triplicate to each racial group. The "shotcaller" will finish his pronouncement with a specific phrase that gets a mass response from his group only. The Latin caller ends his Spanish-language announcement with *"Gracias!"* to which the mass Latino reply is *"a ti!"* — "back at you!" The black shotcaller ends his with "one lup!" (It must be "one love" but I could swear I hear a 'p'.) The white guy finishes his announcement with "woodpile!" and we all yell back "woodpile!" "Woods" is prison slang for whites, shortened from "peckerwoods" (a reversal, obviously, of woodpeckers).

It seems that I offended some sensibilities by going to the bathroom barefoot rather than in flip-flops. Turns out this is quite a no-no — for hygienic reasons, I guess. What was funny was the look of disbelief on the face of the inmate who reproached me for this breach of etiquette. How could anyone not know this most basic rule of incarcerated life?

I didn't even try to explain that not wearing flip-flops was an instinctive attempt to be as unobtrusive as possible. It's easier to slip to the bathroom noiselessly in bare feet, and in my mind, I was being that much more invisible. But what I'm rapidly learning is that the best way not to stand out here is to do exactly what everyone else does exactly the way they do it.

My new bunkie is the stuff of fantasy, truth be told. Dyno's a short ex-Marine with a rocking bod that comes from doing 750 push-ups a day. He should be off killing the Taliban, but on his first leave from basic training he torched an ex-girlfriend's house in a jealous, meth-fueled rage.

I probably should have remembered this bit of information before getting into a discussion about why we invaded Iraq. Dyno flared up quite dramatically at my matter-of-fact contention that Saddam Hussein was not behind 9/11. Oh, boy. Not what they told him in the Marines, evidently.

I realized almost immediately that his decision to join up was sacrosanct to him; perhaps the one life choice that he's ever been proud of. Clearly, he felt very threatened by the notion that he might have been willing to lay down his life for a lie, so I thought it best to reframe my thoughts as mere opinion. After he cooled off, I did suggest, however, that anyone willing to go to war to "defend our freedoms" might remember that one of them is "freedom of speech," and he needn't take it personally if I exercised mine.

So, first lesson about politics in prison — don't discuss politics outside of prison.

It was a little tense there for a day or two, but that blew over. Dyno is basically good-natured, plus I can make him laugh. I think this ability is the secret super-power that will enable me to successfully navigate my way through here unscathed. My greatest coup so far was at breakfast, when someone who noticed how much mail I received asked clear across from the other end of the table if any of it came from a girlfriend. This effectively silenced the other conversations, and everyone turned to hear what I'd say.

"Nope," I answered, stalling for time by reaching for the salt — but really for a salty riposte.

" 'Cause she's the kind of person who can lick everything but a stamp."

Rim-shot.

They laughed so hard that a C.O. told us to "pipe down" on the intercom.

Back at our bunk, Dyno conferred on me the biggest compliment you can get in prison.

"You're all right, Mark. You're all right."

Thorns Without Roses

Now that I've been at Delano a couple of weeks, there's a little more leeway in socializing with non-whites. An older black guy named Rocco noticed me lusting after his 1998 *Vanity Fair* and offered to lend it to me when he finished. We got to talking, and he had such a kindly demeanor that I just had to ask what the hell a man like him was doing in a place like this.

"Alcohol, man. Got me into trouble 30 years ago — that's when I first did time. I got out, and I said, shit, never gonna touch another drop. And I stuck to it too. Got married, had kids, got divorced, got remarried — to the same woman. And then we got divorced again. That's what killed me. 'Cause the second time she filed, she said in court that I hit her, and I swear, I never laid a goddamn hand on her! Never once, on her or our kids!"

He shook his head in that way you shake your head when your own experience seems like something that happened to someone else.

"And the day I got the divorce papers... I got drunk. And guess what I did?"

I shook my head, but I knew what he was about to say.

"I hit her. I went over to her house and hit her."

According to Rocco, she'd dropped the charges. But in California, district attorneys often prosecute anyway when it comes to domestic violence. He'd gotten two years.

We'd spoken as long as I thought we could without it being made note of. No one would have said anything directly, but at one of the weekly meetings of the Woods, the shotcaller might suggest in a general way that we keep our socializing across racial lines to a minimum. He'd say: "Remember, in a riot, they aren't your friends," while staring right at me.

God.

A week or so later, Rocco and I ran into each other washing our faces in adjoining sinks. I thanked him again for the magazine, and he shared a bit of news.

"Guess who wrote me?"

I knew, of course, it could only be his ex-wife.

"What does she want?"

"She wants to visit! Can you believe it?"

I shook my head as if I couldn't, but I could.

The Latin shotcaller is named Loco. His bunk is catty-corner to mine. He's not particularly good-looking but has tons of charisma. His homies are often gathered around his bunk, shooting the shit in Spanish and laughing a lot.

Before I talk about how I got to know Loco, let me back up a bit. When I first got here, a white guy named Big Red (who looks just like his name) came over one day with a question.

"So, are you a writer or something?"

I nodded affirmatively, hoping he didn't follow up with the dreaded inquiry into what I had published. But Red didn't care a fig about my resume. He was simply trying to write a birthday poem for his girlfriend and was stuck at "roses are red, just like me." He wondered if I could help him out. In exchange there'd be three shots of coffee in it for me.

Not exactly W.G.A. minimum, but for someone who hadn't been offered money to write in quite some time, it felt like a three-picture deal with Sony. I sensed that he needed it right away and somehow had the wherewithal to up my fee to five cups of java if I finished it that day.

I've always worked well on a deadline and within a few hours came up with 12 lines that would fill up the inside of a card:

My precious love,
What I would give,

To see you one more time;
To deeply peer,
Into your eyes,
As your heart
Beats next to mine;
I'd gladly trade,
All that I own,
If I could in return;
Obtain one simple
Gift for you,
A rose without a thorn.

I was fairly sure I was not the first poet to come up with the rose-without-a-thorn motif, but Red didn't seem to recognize it — and he had an encyclopedic knowledge of country music. He was quite pleased, and I had coffee for a week.

What I didn't know then is that Red showed the card to his bunkie, who asked if he could use it in a card to his girlfriend, and then later passed it to someone else. Evidently this round robin occurred five or six times, but I only learned about it yesterday when Loco came over, introduced himself, and asked for my opinion about something.

"Could you read this, and tell me what you think is going on with my girlfriend?"

It seemed an awfully intimate request of a complete stranger, but I couldn't think of a reason to say no.

He handed me a letter from his "baby-mama," Nikki.

"Oh, baby, that card was so beautiful! A rose without a thorn! It made me feel so special! I miss you so much! I'm going to put it on the refrigerator and read it every day!"

Incredulous, I turned to Loco.

" 'Rose without a thorn?' Dude, you know I wrote that, right?"

"Of course, I did, dawg! That's why I'm coming to you. You

understand romance and shit!"

Technically, my work had been used without attribution or remuneration. I was supposed to feel disrespected, but I was flattered. Still, I had to pretend otherwise.

"That's not cool, Loco. Red paid me to write that for him. Not for anybody else."

"You're right, Dude. That wasn't cool. I'll make it up to you — what do you want?"

"Seven shots of coffee."

"Deal, dawg."

We shook on it. I started reading the rest of the letter.

In her big rounded letters, with the occasional smiley face for a period, Nikki wrote about living with her *abuela,* a page or so about the baby, and a few paragraphs about "finally" going out for the first time since his birth.

So this was Loco's question, "You think she's seeing another guy?"

I reread the pertinent passages.

"What guy? She doesn't mention a guy."

"She doesn't but... why is she going out then?"

"What do you mean?"

"If she's not looking for someone new, why is she going out?"

"To have fun? To be with her friends?"

The idea that she might have relationships that were unlike hers with him seemed not to have crossed Loco's mind. He was obsessed with the possibility of her infidelity.

"So, you really don't think she's fucking around?"

"Loco, I've never met your girlfriend. All I know is what I read in this one letter, and she seems pretty devoted to you and your kid. I think you're being paranoid."

"I told you, dawg!"

Oh, yeah, I forgot to mention that two of his buddies had drifted over at this point. They were ten years younger than he, and the difference in age showed up in their attitudes.

"Hey, I'm afraid my girlfriend will meet another guy, too!" added Homie One.

"You wish!" said Homie Two. "So she'd stop asking you for money."

The homies high-fived on this one.

"Yeah, all right, so I'm afraid she'll meet another guy," admitted Loco. "But I can't write that to her. Only losers write shit like that."

"So you want to know what I think you should write her instead, is that it?"

"Right!"

Mmh. Perhaps I'd need to renegotiate my price. As if he knew what I was thinking, Loco leaned forward and said low into my ear, "Help me out, and I can get you the best deal on whatever you need when you get out, man. You'll make way more than you did before."

I thanked him for the offer, but told him I was definitely out of that biz. However, I could always use stamps.

"No problem, you got it."

Loco started with a fresh sheet of paper and started writing. "Dear Nikki..."

Then he looked up at me, pen at the ready. I had a feeling that Loco was some big poohbah in the *sureños,* yet here he was, about to take dictation from me.

Even for prison, this was weird. But whatever the circumstances, how many chances in life do you get to play *Cyrano de Bergerac?*

I told him to tell his girlfriend to please get out a spiral notebook and make a log of the baby's progress — when he stood, first steps, first words, etc. She could then send him a report once a month, and he could track his son's progress. I told him to tell her how impressed he was with how well she was taking care of his son, and to always remember to talk to the baby a lot because he'd heard that was good for his little brain.

Loco wrote it all down dutifully, my amanuensis.

I then told Loco to suggest to Nikki that she look into taking a course at the local community college. Just one to start, something that would get her out of the house a bit and give her a way to make new friends.

He resisted this one, so I had to sell it.

"Loco, you can't ask her to sit home with the baby all day and expect her not to get bored out of her mind. You've got to encourage her to have a life besides changing diapers and writing letters to you."

Of course, that's exactly the life he'd expected her to lead. I looked to Homie Two for support, and he obliged.

"Hey, don't you want her to be able to help your son with his homework?"

Just the way he asked that question was a novel in itself, but I couldn't be distracted.

Loco wrote down the suggestion.

"What else?"

"I think that's enough for one letter, don't you? Just add the kind of thing you usually add, you know..."

"That you love her and shit," piped up Homie One.

"Yeah, say something nice," said Homie Two. "Not, 'Don't go to the club, bitch!'"

This made me as well as the homies laugh, but not Loco, who'd probably been thinking of writing just that.

I don't think I caused a real shift in Loco's thinking about Nikki (who, I discovered, is one of three different baby-mamas to his children). More likely, taking my suggestions reflected his desire to try a new strategy to keep her invested in him. Not because he cares so much about the relationship or her or even, sadly, their son, but because he measures himself by how much he can call "mine."

No matter. From inside these walls, I got to blow a fresh breeze of new ideas into the life of a complete stranger, and that's a good day's work.

I hope I'm still here when he gets an answer from Nikki. I wonder if she'll smell a rat.

Whisper

When Dyno shipped out, it meant I could finally move to a bottom bunk. I thought I'd be on my own all through Memorial Day weekend, but coming back from afternoon yard I saw that the top bunk was occupied. There was something familiar about its new resident, but he was taking a nap, and it can be hard to recognize somebody with his eyes closed.

I slipped underneath as quietly as possible, thinking it was always best to put one's most considerate foot forward with a new bunkie. I got lost in a *Newsweek* that Sandra sent (heaven!) and was completely startled when this tall redhead jumped off the bunk above and extended his hand to me.

His name is Perry but as soon as he opened his mouth I remembered his nickname, "Whisper." We'd been at County together and someone had explained to me that his rasp was due to getting stabbed in his throat during a knife-fight years before. He was self-conscious about how he sounded, so didn't talk that much — I don't think we had an entire conversation when we were at County. It was his style of playing cards that I'd noticed there; more precisely, his mastery of shuffling the deck. It turns out that his only legitimate job, years earlier, had been as a dealer in Las Vegas (cards not drugs — that came later).

Although I met him in the gay dorms, I don't think Whisper is gay, at least not the conventional sense. We've only had one conversation that veered into personal territory, and he seems to have an ongoing "thing" with a transgender girl who also cycles in and out of prison. Whisper freely admits that his primary relationship is with heroin, and being incarcerated at least gives him a break from the daily hustle required to feed that particular dragon.

That's pretty common, actually. For many of these guys, prison just represents a different set of stresses than those experienced on the street — and some of them don't seem to have a strong preference for one experience over the other. That should not be interpreted to mean that life in prison is anything besides dismal; rather that life on the outside is just a lighter shade of gray for many of them.

While most inmates, like Whisper and me, just want to keep their heads down and do their time, some seem to thrive on the politics. "Chainsaw" is one of those men. He is less mean-looking than his name sounds, but still plenty mean. And pretty good looking (a taller version of Dyno), which is annoying.

Being a politician, he has been strolling around the dorm in anticipation of being named the next white shotcaller upon the departure of the current one. He's already asked me twice if I'm a skinhead, although it's obvious I'm not. He was also very curious about where I sold and to whom.

"Mostly Hollywood," I told him.

"And West Hollywood, too, I bet. Lot of queers there," he noted snidely.

I shrugged, trying to be a casual.

"I went where the money was."

He snickered and walked away.

Understandably, this exchange made me very nervous, but Whisper calmed me down. A little.

"I've seen that type before. Rich kid who gets in trouble and tries to pretend like he's not scared as shit by playing the bully. He's no skinhead. He just shaves his head and talks tough."

Athough at that meeting of the Woods, It was Chainsaw who had brought up how we need to be ready in case "something went off."

Whisper laughed. "I *guarantee* you... he's the type you'll find huddled under a bunk in a race riot. I guarantee you."

Right next to me, basically.

May or May Not

Chainsaw did indeed ascend to shotcaller, which seems to have partially satisfied his need to feel important. Thank God he bunks on the second floor, and I can avoid him most of the time.

It helps considerably that a new arrival has taken quite a shine to me. His name is Tim, but he goes by Thumper. That's a pretty good nickname for someone who looks like a welterweight boxer. He's about 5'9", defined and tattooed, with a crooked nose that gives his face just the right amount of off-kilter handsomeness. His brown eyes are darkly Slavic, but his smile sparkles like he's in a Pepsodent commercial. He is seriously sexy; the kind of man who could spend an hour chatting up guests at a party and leave every woman — and quite a few men — thinking they'd had a "moment" with him. After several such "moments" with him, I have concluded that what really turns him on is seeing how much he turns you on.

Perhaps that's the definition of narcissism, but I tend to be very forgiving of a high level of self-regard in a beautiful man. (An ugly narcissist, now *that's* unacceptable.) Besides, he's a very nice narcissist — at least to me. I guess not to everybody else, or he wouldn't be here.

The *CliffsNotes* version of Thumper's story is basically Michael Corleone in *The Godfather,* except Romanian. The way he tells it, his auto body shop-owning father got in trouble with some Serbian loan sharks, and Thumper, all of 17, was torn from a golden-boy captain-of-the-football-team life and forced to work off his father's debts by engaging in some pretty shady stuff, which may or may not have included loan-sharking, jewel-heisting, and "drug-trafficking." That's as specific as I can get on why he is here, which may or may not have something to do with the phrase "Albanian Mafia."

Thumper's attentiveness is so pronounced that even Whisper asked if "anything was going on between you two." He winked as he asked, because he knew of course, that it would be unthinkable to be anything but chaste here. But I was relieved to know that I wasn't conjuring something out of my own wishful-thinking crush.

Of course, what is "going on," exactly, remains a bit of a mystery.

I have noticed a lot of guys here engaged in the kind of *sotto voce tête-a-tête* that you rarely see between two men in "real" life outside of a football huddle. I think it's the shipping-out-tomorrow nature of Delano. You figure out quickly if someone is an ally, and intimacy can develop fast, homoerotic or otherwise.

I don't know how severe a wise-guy Thumper actually was on the outside, but it seems enough to have earned him a vaguely menacing reputation. Although it's completely at odds with his affability around me, I'm grateful for it. Ever since we started hanging out, Chainsaw has definitely been spending far less time sniffing around in this neck of the woods.

Let Me Tell You

Whisper arrived after I did but left before me. That was a surprise. In principle, it's first-in, first-out, but perhaps my departure has been delayed because I have to go to one of the four facilities that houses HIV+ inmates. Not that we're segregated once we get there, but the AIDS doctors who are willing to work in the prison system are available only in these four places. (Frankly, I wouldn't mind if we were segregated. It would be far less nerve-wracking.)

In fact, HIV is almost certainly what I have in common with the two gay men I've met here, Art and Scott. Not that we'd say that out loud, even to each other. I just see them at Pill Call every day, and that's a sure tip-off. That everyone else doesn't know it, too, reflects the fact that so many men are in line for psych meds that we don't stick out. Which reminds me of the old joke from the '80s

"What's the hardest thing about having AIDS?"
"Convincing your parents you're Haitian."

We just have to pretend to be in line for our happy pills, and we're good to go.

Speaking of grinning sociopaths, Loco did show up with a response from Nikki, who, as I predicted, could not have been more shocked by "his" letter than if a Martian had written it in green blood. This does not mean she wasn't pleased, though. In fact, she was thrilled. This, in turn, put a smile on Loco's face, although I have no idea how he'll sustain the charade. He asked me to dictate another letter, but I told him he was on his own. (The choices you get to make when you can finally buy your own coffee!)

Since Thumper wangled a kitchen job, I see him less often. That's probably a good thing, as some of our conversations had become a bit intense. He was talking about moving together to Argentina when we got out. When he found out about my forgery skills, he proposed all kinds of ways to make a buck, and I mean literally "make" a buck. He would spin these fantasies sitting on my bunk, allowing his torso to completely lean against my knees. To boot, he showed me a letter he received from a guy he'd gotten really "tight with" in Orange County lock-up. It was about as close to a love letter as you could possibly get without spelling it out explicitly. ("God, man, I really miss hanging out with you — more than you can imagine," and "I'm getting out in December, and I'm hoping we can spend Christmas together.")

It wasn't clear why Thumper was telling me any of this. Did he want me to spell out my sexuality for him, so he could then say, "Oh, my God, I thought so!" If we were anywhere else, I would have, but this is obviously a place where you err on the side of utmost caution.

Art is a quiet Latino around my age. I extended myself to him because he is shunned by the other Latinos. It's not that he's particularly effeminate, just that he doesn't try to hide being gay. He pretends their cold shoulder doesn't bug him, but I can tell he's been dealing with this kind of shit his whole life and is just plain weary. At first he was suspicious of my kindness, then opened up a little when Loco said hi to us when I was sitting on his bunk.

Art described a milquetoast life, working at a grocery store and living with his Mom. The deal was that he took care of her, and she didn't comment on the bottle of wine he drank every night. Then she died and left him a little money. He treated himself to new furniture, a vacation, some nice clothes. But what really did him in was discovering French wine. When the money ran out, he tried to go back to the cheap stuff but couldn't. "I would have two sips of *Franzia,* or whatever, and then go out and buy some *Pouilly-Fuissé.* And when I couldn't afford it anymore,

I'd shoplift it. I'd sew up the sleeves of a coat and put it over my shoulders, and just slide the bottles in there."

I thought this was pretty inventive.

"Yeah. The judge said exactly the same thing."

There were attempts to get sober, but each relapse seemed to bring out riskier behavior. "I'm a friggin' kleptomaniac when I drink, let me tell you." (That's his favorite phrase, "let me tell you.")

"Let me tell you, if you're going to steal shit, don't do it drunk. 'Cause they can smell the alcohol on your breath."

I tried not to laugh, but couldn't help myself. Then Art started to laugh, too — I had the distinct sensation that it was the first time that had happened in a while.

Scott, who's about 35, has the kind of looks that work a lot better from a distance than close up, where his queeny personality ruins them. He likes to read his poetry for children out loud to me. You'd think he was standing in a kindergarten classroom, trying to keep the kids entranced with a lot of swooping hand gestures and flamboyant animal characters. To put it in the gayest words possible — It's just not a good look for where we are.

He's a bit cagey about how he got here, and tends to address any sensitive question in ornate paragraphs peppered with phrases like, "It was just a big misunderstanding." He's so thin that I'm sure his offense was meth-related. But I'm not pushing for details because he talks too much and too loudly as it is.

This situation reminds me of Eddie Hudson back in high school, when I tried to keep our friendship confined to the Drama Society and avoided him in the cafeteria at lunch. He finally called me on it and I had to apologize. I probably would have gotten more grief from the jocks back then, but they were in awe of how I could pull up a chair at the girls' table and entertain them for 20 minutes. (Oh, my God, everybody was so naïve in 1972. That comfort with the opposite sex confirmed exactly what they thought it disproved!)

I guess that's why I feel a little uncomfortable about my discomfort around Scott. It seems cowardly. On the other hand, if you're going to be a coward, this is the place to do it.

Bully

Yesterday afternoon, Thumper was at work and Scott was at my bunk, reciting one of his children's stories about a talking crocodile. When he first shared his work with me, I'd made the mistake of praising one inventive turn-of-phrase, not realizing that was as good as it would get. Now he seems deaf to any criticism, not to mention blind to all cues that perhaps he might fly a bit lower under the gaydar. I swear, I could be frantically waving a checkered pink flags an inch from his face, and all he would say is, "Oh, you're going to *love* this one."

There are some things that ostensibly heterosexual men in prison don't do, and one of them is read children's poetry out loud. You can share rap lyrics about having to murder your own cousin, but rhymes about Albert the Alligator — not so much. Two straight guys in here are more likely to have sex with each other, frankly.

Ever since Thumper's been working, I've noticed Chainsaw lurking around more. And as Scott was going on and on, I got this sinking feeling we were being watched. I was right. He was staring at us from the second floor.

I decided to cut off Scott as soon as he finished the stanza that he was spouting madly, but Chainsaw showed up first. By then even Scott knew to shut up.

Chainsaw got to the point.

"I have to talk to you guys."

"What's up?" I asked, as butchly as possible.

"There's a rumor going around that you two are homosexual and HIV-positive."

Homosexual? I thought. What is this, 1965?

A thousand ripostes popped into my head, all sarcastic and bitchy, right out of *The Boys in the Band*. But Scott responded first, rolling out the denial he'd no doubt rehearsed and memorized the day he was sentenced.

"Well, I don't know *who* said such a thing or why, but I am *not* homosexual and the meds I take are for colorectal cancer." Although the denial reeked of inauthenticity, it seemed to be what Chainsaw wanted to hear. He cared less about whether we were actually gay than showing everybody that he had the right to ask whether we were.

I'm not particularly brave, but I wasn't about to give into his petty tyranny, either. I answered the question with a question.

"Who wants to know and why do they want to know it?"

This annoyed him, but he couldn't think of how not to answer it.

"Well... one of the Latins said something, and as the white shotcaller, I have to know whether to make an issue out of it."

"Well, you don't. I don't give a shit if any of the Latins or anyone else thinks I'm gay or HIV+. They can say whatever they want."

This attitude, of course, did not comport with Chainsaw's worldview, and you could see his inner logic system overloading. In his mind, no straight man would ever be indifferent to being perceived as gay. Further, a gay man could at least have the decency to be ashamed about it. My refusal to agree to either premise infuriated him.

Chainsaw so much as admitted how vague his motives were in asking.

"Listen, I'm the head of the Woods, and I need to know what's up with the other Woods."

"Why? So you can defend me? I haven't been attacked. The only one here who ever hassles me is you."

Chainsaw sputtered.

"Well, AIDS is infectious, so I have a right to know about

that!"

I knew I might regret what came out of my mouth next, but I just couldn't resist.

"No, you really don't. Unless you're intending to have sex with me, it's none of your business."

Scott let out an audible gasp at that one. He literally started backing away, and then bumped smack dab into a lanky redhead carrying a duffle bag.

"Sorry," squeaked out Scott, who then scrambled away faster than a cartoon roadrunner.

The new arrival was unperturbed. He was fixated on the man who looked like he was about to deck me.

"Chainsaw?"

It took a second or two for Chainsaw to retrieve his name.

"Scooter, right?"

"Skeeter."

"Oh, shit, sorry, man. Skeeter..." Our situation was impossible to describe in a few seconds, and Chainsaw was at a loss for words.

Skeeter didn't pick up on a thing. Instead, he looked at the little piece of paper in his hand.

"Hey, you know where D-126 is? Top?"

Oh, for crying out loud. That was my bunk. This kid was Whisper's replacement.

I lifted my finger and pointed to the bed.

"You're my new bunkie."

I shook his hand, looking directly at Chainsaw. *Watch me spread AIDS through casual contact, you ignorant dickwad.*

Chainsaw glared right back, not even looking at Skeeter as he asked:

"You got your cards?"

"Of course,."

"Come find me upstairs later. We'll hang out."

He gave me an "I'll-deal-with-you-later" look, and returned

to the second floor.

I realized immediately that I had five minutes to make an impression that would counteract whatever bullshit he was about to hear from Chainsaw.

"So you guys were together at..."

"Modesto."

"Was he shotcaller there, too?"

"Chainsaw is the shotcaller here?"

"Yup."

"Cool! No, we didn't really have a shotcaller at County. But he and I hung out. Played cards a lot."

He was trying to act casual, but you could tell that he had a very serious case of hero-worship, which I found ironic, considering the information Chainsaw had just been after from me.

He'd almost finished putting away his things. I had to think quickly.

"You need anything? I would have killed for some coffee and toothpaste when I got here."

His face lit up.

"Really? I'd pay you back."

"Actually I owe some to the white kitty. Why don't you give it to Chainsaw for me? If he gives it back to you, then I'll at least have covered my ass."

I actually owed nothing to the kitty, but it seemed a good way to keep Chainsaw off-balance.

"By the way," I asked as if inquiring about the weather, "do you know how he got his nickname? We've talked a few times, but I've never asked him."

"His real name is Charlie. But his father owns a sawmill, so, 'Chainsaw...'"

"That makes sense."

Skeeter almost instantly realized that his eagerness to show me that he was close to Chainsaw had caused him to reveal a secret. The last thing Chainsaw wanted was for anybody to know his tough prison moniker was unearned.

Skeeter lowered his voice.

"But don't call him that... 'Charlie.' I probably shouldn't have mentioned it."

I shrugged, as if I'd already forgotten it, but of course, I found this little bit of information reassuring. Charlie isn't nearly as scary as "Chainsaw." Definitely worth a tube of toothpaste.

King of the Jungle

The average stay here is about eight weeks, and around week six or seven, everyone starts looking for their name on a list that is posted every Friday of upcoming transfers. Everyone is glad to be moving on, if only because the "mainline" offers far more privileges than a reception center like Delano. Most guys are impatient to finally smoke again, but what I look forward to most is a decent library and being able to order a radio. With any luck, I'll be able to get a local NPR station.

Guys who have been through the system a few times (which is nearly everyone) sure have their preferences as far as where they are headed, though. Their reactions range from a whoop of triumph to abject disappointment, reminding me of nothing more than my friends' reactions back in high school upon opening their college acceptance/rejection letters. I've kept this wry observation to myself, of course. Somehow I don't think, "gee, this reminds me of when my friend Karen didn't get into Cornell in 1976!" would be much appreciated.

There is an absolutely stunning black guy here whose nickname is "Monster" because he's built like a brick shithouse. I've never seen a man do so many pull-ups in my life (off the underside of the steel stairwells). He's also got an incredible smile, which he once flashed at me when he caught me enjoying a particular groove on one of the three radio stations they play every afternoon. "So you like Usher, do you, Mark?" It was both an affectionate tease and an oblique warning that perhaps I should be little less overt about my R&B proclivities. You just never know what a peckerwood will make an issue out of here, after all.

Monster got his assignment when I did, and was quite happy to be going to Avenal — which is where Dyno went, I think.

Next to my name was C.I.M-Chino, which I announced with a naïve hope that it was equally good news. Monster's normally effervescent smile was suddenly AWOL, replaced by a sympathetic grimace.

"What's wrong with Chino?" I asked.

"Nothing wrong. Chino's fine."

There were no pearly whites accompanying that reassurance. Not good.

Then it occurred to me that maybe Chino had a bad reputation for black men; perhaps the guards there were particularly racist or something. So I turned to Aram, a young Armenian who was doing time with his father, no less. (Well, he called him his father, but they didn't look alike. That could have just been more identity theft.) Aram liked me because I'd walked with his "Dad" around the track a few times at yard, and we'd spoken in French, which he knew from living in Beirut many years ago.

"Aram, you know anything about Chino?" I asked.

He scrunched up his face.

"It's just kind of... shot-out."

I actually wasn't sure what that meant.

"Decrepit!" someone else threw out.

"Smells likes cowshit!" added another voice from the peanut gallery.

Monster motioned me over.

"You'll be fine. Chino is only an hour from L.A. Your friends can visit. And it's the same *Eyewitness News* that you're used to."

Monster and I had joked about this once in the day room when we watched the local Bakersfield *Action News*. I told him I missed seeing reports from neighborhoods I used to drive through back in L.A.

I felt emboldened to make a suggestion that I'd been carrying around in my back pocket for a while.

"Monster... you ever been to Universal Studios?"

"No, I don't think so. Just Disneyland."

"Even better. Did you go to the *Pirates of the Caribbean?* Not the ride, the show."

"The show?"

"Well, they have these big live-action shows at the parks, you know, like *Aladdin* and *Pirates of the Caribbean*. And they cast athletic actors with lots of charisma to swing from ropes and do stunts, like swashbucklers. You should just try something like that. You'd be a natural."

Monster probably understood that this was a roundabout way of me giving him a compliment informed by sexual attraction, but he also sensed correctly that I was being totally sincere. He *would* be a natural.

"Are you saying you think I could steal the show instead of BMW's?"

That smile again.

"Yes, I am. And they won't arrest you afterwards, either."

He put his hand on my shoulder — normally a no-no, but one he could get away with.

"I like that part of it. I like that part a lot."

At lunch that day, Monster swept through asking for any of our uneaten extras — an orange here, a piece of bread there.

"I need every calorie! Gotta feed the beast!"

He winked at me as he said it, already *Tarzan*.

Showdown

I'm writing this from the benches at the front of the dorm. It's four in the morning, and the buses to take me and a few others to Chino will be here in about an hour.

Until yesterday, things were fairly uneventful except for the uncomfortable feeling that every interaction I had was being reported by Skeeter to Chainsaw. I did make use of knowing I was being listened to, though. Thumper asked me about the circumstances that led to my being here, and I told him about Luke's death being the starting point of everything. Pretending to lower my voice, but in fact projecting it just a little (an old acting trick) I said:

"That's why I didn't like answering Chainsaw's question. My brother was gay, and he died of AIDS, so I'm a little sensitive about the whole topic." I knew that Skeeter would breathlessly share this bit of gossip as soon as he got the chance, and that my sidestepping "explanation" would irritate Chainsaw all the more. (At this point, that's all I really want to do — fuck with his head.)

It was also the first time I'd used the word "gay" with Thumper. I figured if he wanted to use it as an opening to broach the topic, he could, but he took no such opportunity. He's not a big fan of Chainsaw, though, and did say (after Skeeter had gone upstairs), "You know, I always got your back, bro."

Of course, to have my back he can't be in the kitchen, which is several buildings away and where he was working this morning.

On Sunday, we get razors on the first floor for about ten minutes. Everyone has to turn in his ID card to get one in exchange, and they are carefully counted. How anybody manages to not return one is beyond me, but they do, because the sharp edges evidently show up in crude weapons.

In any case, I just wanted to shave off my stubble, and found myself competing for sinks downstairs. You really don't want to be jostling a skinhead who is rendering his scalp completely bald. Since the guys upstairs get their razors on different days, a bunch of us downstairs rushed up there to use their sinks, two of which are located outside of the bathroom. (Installed to deal with over-crowding, no doubt.) I did my best to shave quickly, but it was a messy affair with so many men trying to do the same thing at the same time, made worse by the countdown, which was announced on the loudspeakers ("you've got five minutes left, inmates") al-most as soon as the razor was in your hand.

I finished shaving and headed toward the stairs. Then, from behind, Chainsaw barked:

"Olmsted!"

Uh-oh. I hadn't even been thinking of Chainsaw being up here. I turned, slowly.

"What?"

"You left a fucking mess. What do you think this is, dude? You think you can just go and leave a mess in someone's else's sink?"

"What are you talking about?"

He pointed to the sink. There was a ring of hair around it, left behind by the drained water. It belonged to all of us who'd shaved, which I probably shouldn't have pointed out with such a dismissive tone in my voice.

"That's not just mine, and you know it."

"Looks to me like you were the last one to use it. So you should clean it up."

This was the kind of moment I'd feared would happen. Chain-saw knew I was shipping out, and wanted to show everybody else he'd humiliated the "AIDS faggot" or whatever he called me be-hind my back. I kept hoping Thumper would appear, but he was chopping vegetables (or whatever he did) in the kitchen.

Then it occurred to me that if Chainsaw had been spreading the rumor that I was HIV+, he might suddenly accuse me of endangering everybody if I nicked my face-making me a "danger" to use the same sink. I was better off just wiping it out thoroughly with my towel. Then I turned to him with as much defiance as I could muster, and delivered my shortest and least eloquent speech ever.

"There."

Several of the other inmates were watching now; it was tense. Chainsaw must have flashed back to ninth grade at Modesto Christian High, when the bully was still one of the bullied. (Skeeter had let slip something about a P.E. teacher who made his life miserable.) This would explain his next attempt to punish me.

"You know, I think this shows a lot of disrespect. I think maybe you owe us 123 burpies." Owe "us?" I could hear no murmur of support from the onlookers — if anything, they were on my side. Everyone knew I was no troublemaker, and more than a few had come to me for shots of coffee or stamps. I knew the punishment was arbitrary, not to mention dangerous. That many burpies (squat-thrusts basically) on a 44-year-old who hadn't been to the gym in years could induce a heart attack.

Instead, without my eyes leaving his, I simply wiped the sink again in the most perfunctory manner possible. This time I let some sarcasm creep in.

"I'm sorry. I guess I missed a spot. Now I'm done."

This was a good line to walk away on, and I did just that, brushing right past him.

He called out my name once again, but without conviction. I kept walking, holding up my razor. "Gotta return this." It was the truth, which allowed Chainsaw to save just enough face to back down. If he'd forced me to get into trouble with the guard for returning it late, he would have definitely lost the crowd.

I walked down the stairs and to the guard box where the razors were being collected. I didn't hear anyone following me down the steps, but wasn't about to look back, either.

When the guard handed me back my ID, he paused.

"Olmsted. Hang on."

He looked down at a clipboard.

"You ship out in the morning. Early."

This was one of the nice guards, Winkowski. He was young and pale and seemed ill-suited for this job. I'd always seen him as more of a bank teller, the kind who keeps getting robbed in an old Western.

I thanked him for the info, and returned to my bunk.

Skeeter was there, following me with his beady little eyes and no doubt hoping to report back to Chainsaw that our encounter had made me cry.

Instead, I opened my locker, and told Skeeter with as much studied casualness as I could muster that I was shipping out.

"You want the rest of my coffee?"

Skeeter was one of those poor inmates who didn't even get an occasional letter, much less any money on his books. He couldn't afford to refuse anything, and I knew it. But no doubt he was afraid that Chainsaw would find out it was my coffee, and claim it for the white kitty — or maybe even himself.

"I don't know," he answered lamely.

That's when Thumper returned from his shift.

"Hey, Tim. If I give you the rest of my coffee, will you share it with Skeeter?"

"Sure, Mark."

I handed him the jar, my eyes staying right on Skeeter.

"And he can share it with Charlie, if he wants."

"Who's Charlie?" asked Thumper.

"Did I say Charlie? I meant Chainsaw."

Skeeter shrunk a bit. Sharing this little secret was my parting gift to Thumper, just in case Chainsaw thought about mucking with him next.

Later I told Thumper what had happened, although somehow it sounded less fraught with danger in the retelling than when it occurred.

He put an arm around my shoulders.

"I'm gonna miss you."

"I'm gonna miss you, too."

"Don't forget. Argentina. I got plans for us."

I didn't contradict him. And even though he asked me to wake him, I just left a note for him when it came time to gather my things. I included my Mom's address in New York, which seemed far enough away to be safe.

I wonder if I'll ever really understand what passed between Thumper and me. But it'll be fun to think of him on the bus and to fantasize about our life in Buenos Aires, even though he might as well have said the moon.

Dear Sandra - I

Just a note to tell you I arrived at Chino yesterday, but the war-den evidently didn't get the memo that I required a penthouse suite, so my deluxe private accommodations don't seem to be ready. (Translation — There are no free beds in the orientation dorm.) So I have been temporarily housed in a wing called Syc-amore West, in a cell like the one I shared with Mack that first week in Delano.

My new cellie is nice enough, but I'd rather wait until I've reached my new dorm to write about what it's like here. (Some things you'd rather just describe when you are seeing them in the rear-view mirror.)

You can post this on the blog if you want, so those who check in daily won't worry at the temporary silence. (I know I must have thousands of readers by now — nay, millions! Hello, legions of slavish fans and admirers! I know you hang on every word, but you may have a small breather to pay some attention to your personal life. And my sister's fingers could probably use a break.)

Will write in a few.

Love, Bro

Dear Sandra - II

You'll see from the return address that I am writing to you from Birch Hall, which is Chino's protective custody dorm. So I am no longer at Sycamore.

Praise fucking Jesus. That was definitely the longest week of my life.

It was all I could do to keep a casual tone in the little note I sent you when I first got here. I knew that if I wrote anything longer, I would have betrayed how utterly scared I was, and then instead of just me being in a state of panic, you and Erica and Mom would have been in one, too.

I am now in a dorm that is a lot like County — a mixture of gays, the transgendered, and older men. So as you read about these unpleasant last eight days, just remember it's behind me now.

Love, Bro

Friendless Stranger

On the bus from Delano, I sat behind a chatty black guy who was telling his nervous seatmate — a newbie like me — that Chino has its own intake/reception process, meaning the first two weeks are spent in an orientation dorm called Cedar Hall. But when I got up to the intake coordinator, he said "Cedar is full, you're getting housed somewhere else tonight." He scanned a sheet on a clipboard, wrote something down, and handed me a slip of paper. He told me to give it to another guard down the hall, who would escort me to my cell.

I was taken to Sycamore West, which consists of three tiers of two-man cells along a long corridor, facing the dreariest, dirtiest windows I had ever seen. I thought where I'd been with Mack was oppressive, but it turns out that cellblocks built in the 1990s, like Delano, were designed to make it hard for inmates in different cells to communicate with each other. The result was thick walls between cells and a fairly quiet block. But Sycamore is a much older design; stacked cages like San Quentin or Attica, with acoustics to match.

The noise, simply put, was overwhelming. Everyone on the block seemed to be yelling from his cell and carrying on, each voice ricocheting and echoing in complete cacophony. My first thought was that it would be impossible for anyone to serve any length of time there without going crazy.

Indeed, few are there for more than 120 days, because that's the maximum time that can be given for a sentence to a Special Disciplinary Unit. I learned that on my fourth day there; that I had landed in an SDU. This was the place you had time added to your term because you were caught fighting or found with contraband or refused to follow a guard's order. Usually 30, 60 or 90 days would be added to your sentence, up to four months. Anything more serious was likely to land you a new charge, complete with a new arrest (inside the jail) and a new term to start when you finished the one you were already serving.

My cellie's name was Drifter. He was another tattooed skinhead, around 30, originally from Mississippi. The hint of an overbite prevented him from being handsome, but a lean, defined body more than made up for it.

Not only had the intake guard informed me that my stay in the wing was temporary, but Drifter also said he'd had a succession of temporary cellies. For the first two days, every time a guard appeared, I was sure he was coming to take me to another dorm. By the third night, I was becoming afraid I'd gotten lost in the system. With growing dread, I started to get used to the routine.

Every morning, the "keeper of the keys" for each race would go through a roll call, yelling out the name of each inmate on the three tiers belonging to his race. It was ridiculously early, around 5:30 or so, and you would try to just keep one eye open long enough to yell out, "Wood present!" when your name was called. The blacks and the Latins then did their own roll calls, and finally you could go back to sleep until breakfast. The sole point of this exercise, I gathered, was to let the other races know that yours was ready to fight at the crack of dawn in case they were planning to start something when the cells opened and we went to breakfast.

Throughout the day, we endured a military-like enforcement of call-outs. Whenever a guard appeared on a walkway, the lookout in the first cell would yell, "Guard on the Tier!" and everybody on all three floors would be required to yell back, "Guard on the Tier!" as loudly as they could. When the C.O. completed his or her rounds, you'd hear "Guard off the Tier!" and you'd have to yell back "Thank you!" at full volume. If you didn't participate, you might be reprimanded by the head of your racial group. It reminded me of Baathist party members who didn't dare stop clapping first when Saddam Hussein gave a speech. It was headache-inducing to shout like that so many times a day, and deafening every time to hear it.

The purpose of the initial warning that a guard was apporaching was clear enough. If you were doing something illicit, like making pruno, then you knew to hide it fast. But the constant shouting back struck me as an egregious form of self-punishment. Everybody hated it, but no one dared deviate from established prison culture. And the guards certainly don't discourage any system whereby the inmates enforce their own discipline.

To make matters worse, there had been a big fight just before I arrived. Someone had been sent to the hospital, so we were on lockdown for my first three days. That means we were in our cells for 23 hours each day. Even the meals were brought in, handed through the bars of the cell on Styrofoam trays or in paper bags. We called that "room service."

After each meal, you threw containers and empty milk cartons out through the bars. The floor served as a giant trash receptacle, swept up several times a day by porters — a prized job because it got you out of your cell. I found it depressing to see the trash, much of it chucked out from the upper floors. The overall effect was incredibly dehumanizing; loud and dirty, like a zoo. Everyone else seemed desensitized to the noise and garbage, but I couldn't imagine getting used to it.

At first I didn't think I'd get to know Drifter, because at any moment the coordinator would come to his senses and pluck me out of there, but after a few days I had no choice. Soon enough, I discovered that he was more than happy to talk about himself, probably in direct proportion to how little anyone had ever listened to him.

His story was all kinds of fishy though — full of one too

many instances of awfully bad luck. He supposedly "borrowed" a friend's car and had been accused of stealing it, then missed a court date because he had to go back to Mississippi for a family emergency, and before you knew it, had "absconded." Then there he was one day, putting up drywall, and the cops were at the door and he was being extradited to California.

He was the type who unwittingly tipped off every lie by adding, " Can you believe it?" each time he told one. I wanted to answer, "No, I can't, actually," but instead I just nodded sympathetically. This was not the place to point out obvious mendacity. Some cellies — much bigger and taller than I — might have felt disrespected, but I took it as Drifter seeking my approval by trying to make himself look good.

Drifter only received mail from a devout Christian grandmother who sent him newsy little notes filled with Bible verses and suggested prayers. One letter included a photograph announcing the arrival of his newborn daughter. Doing the math, it seemed like Drifter had knocked the baby's mother up and left her stranded. Like a good Southern girl, though, she knew enough to come show her respects to Drifter's Mamaw with the new bundle of joy. "Don't worry," reassured his grandmother. "I don't give her cash. I took her to the Piggly-Wiggly to buy some diapers, though."

The evidence of her street-wisdom might have buoyed Drifter more, but she also enclosed some kind of prayer card sent to her by the *700 Club* acknowledging her $10 contribution. Drifter didn't have to tell me how much more he could have used that money than Pat Robertson.

After finding out he was a Dad, Drifter seemed to feel guilty for not being there in Mississippi, and he spent even more time on his hobby-sketching a mural completely in pencil on the far wall of the cell. He created an undersea vista of fish and fauna that wasn't half-bad, actually. I knew it had to be against the rules, but Miss Dade was the only guard who seemed to notice, and that was to check on its progress. A slightly overweight, plain woman in her '30s who smelled of cigarettes and coffee, she came by daily to converse with Drifter. Every day they had a similar exchange:

"Look, Miss Dade, can you see what I added?" asked Drifter.

She would peer through the bars.

"That fish is new, the striped one."

"And look, this coral reef over here."

"A reef?"

"Well, not a whole one, but these are... whatchamacall..."

"Anemones," I offered.

"Right. Those," added Drifter, afraid to mispronounce it if he repeated it.

I decided to try out a little joke on Miss Dade.

"You know that saying, 'with friends like that, who needs anemones?'"

In typical guard fashion, Miss Dade suppressed a laugh, but you could tell she thought it was funny.

Drifter gave me the side-eye, and I could see that he didn't like sharing the spotlight with me. He'd been flirting with Miss Dade for a while, I gathered, and didn't really want any competition.

That afternoon was the first time he asked me what I was taking pills for, anyway. There was an edge to the question.

"Prostate cancer," I said. "Keeps it in remission."

His curiosity pretty much ended there, but he was definitely starting to wonder.

Four days in, we got off lockdown. This meant that I got to know a few of the guys when we ate in the mess hall, and they got to know me. Rebel, the white shotcaller, was one of those charismatic men that the other white inmates looked up to — particularly Drifter. It was another Chainsaw/Skeeter relationship. They ate together, and after that lunch, Drifter was definitely cooler to me.

You could see he felt conflicted about the nudge from Rebel

to make sure we didn't get too chummy. I don't think anybody had ever encouraged him to think of himself as an artist, as I had, and it made it difficult for him to dislike me. But when a book my sister had of my poetry arrived, his curiosity got the best of him, and he asked to look at it.

"Mmh," was the closest he got to a compliment, but he read through the poems attentively.

All week, Drifter and Rebel had been dropping kites to each other about some mysterious project, and then on Friday, the porter smuggled over a package under his sweatshirt. It was a bag of Pruno. Drifter announced that he was going to get drunk.

I didn't want any, but it struck me as incredibly rude that he didn't offer. After his tongue loosened a little, even he felt weird about it, and said something about this being Rebel's personal stash, and he "couldn't" share. Ironically, of course, I was still his de facto drinking buddy, because I was the only person he could talk to while he was imbibing.

This is how I discovered that Drifter took the Aryan Nations shit very seriously. Evidently, he considered himself a "soldier," and had allowed shanks to be hidden in his cell by a higher-up in the gang — I suspect Rebel. The knives had been discovered during a search and 120 days had been tacked onto his sentence as a sanction. He finished his little story like this, "Yup. That's how I landed in Stickamore."

Stick-a-what?

I must have been the only inmate in Chino who didn't know that "Sycamore" was referred to this way. It's just a pun, I told myself. Ha, ha. Ignore the fact that your cellie was just talking about being caught with sharp stabbing implements, and that he's dying to show off to the redneck gang leader he hero-worships.

Luckily, Drifter was a happy drunk. He talked a lot, then grew silent. He asked to read through my poems again and dozed off with them on his chest.

I hadn't realized that Saturday night was Talent Night. From our cells, we heard the head from each race call us out in a round robin to sing a song, tell a joke or recite an original poem. The whites, blacks, and Latins all took turns quite politely. It was a rare show of complete intra-racial civility. I was all set to read one of my poems, but Rebel only called on Drifter, who asked me if he could read one of mine. He didn't really wait for an answer. He clearly had one already picked out and was going to read it whether I "gave" it to him or not.

It was a dark poem, one of my best, well-suited for this crowd. To my surprise, he read it well:

Strange Friend
Neither impatient nor loud,
he was very easy to ignore, at first.
But he made himself felt
in the deep of my gut,
not content, after all, in the shadows,
where he lurked,
unseen by most
but not by me.

If I could not ignore him,
perhaps I could know him;
make a friend of this friendless stranger.
The friendless are eager
to be friended.

So now I have this nameless friend,
a friend for life, he likes to say.
He drapes himself about me,
and listens with both ears,
so patiently.
So patient.

But my new friend is jealous,
as new friends sometimes are,
I must turn old friends away,
even show my love the door.
My friend has made it clear
there's room for only one-
including me.

Now that no one's left,
from the life I've left behind,
my friend declares it time
for dreaming.
My friend is wise.
By closing them, my eyes are opened.

The morning light springs hope eternal.
But horizon light is setting sun,
my tunnel's end has come.
Hope falls eternal.

If I knew his name was death,
I did not know I knew it.
But it can't be said,
I did not choose
to not know
what I should have.

That the friendless
are friendless
for cause,
and the bliss of ignorance
is no bliss
at all.

Drifter got a good round of applause while I stupidly waited for him to mention that I'd written it. Instead, he basked in the reaction, quite pleased that everyone assumed the poem was his.

I knew I could have yelled out that I wanted to read something, but I also knew the poem's style would be so similar that it would effectively blow Drifter's cover, or worse, they'd think I'd taken it from him. It seemed far more politic to just keep my mouth shut. After all, I knew whom all that applause had really been for.

When it was Rebel's turn, he offered a joke; but prefaced it with a little shout-out, "Hey, Drifter, tell this to one to your cellie, he'll appreciate it."

Uh-oh.

"What's the definition of a best friend?"

"What, dawg?" Drifter yelled out.

"A best friend is someone who gets two blow jobs from his girlfriend, just so he can bring the second one back to you."

Everyone roared, of course. I would have laughed hard too, if he hadn't basically called me a faggot in front of the whole wing.

I didn't sleep very well that night, but after breakfast I was clear on what to do. We were still on a modified lockdown, so were escorted in pairs to the showers. When Drifter was taking his, I leaned over to the guard.

"Listen, Miss Dade, I'm in a bind. Drifter's pretty much an Aryan Nations guy, and I'm gay and HIV+. I think he's figured it out. It's starting to feel like any minute I'm going to get the shit kicked out of me, or worse. You've got to move me!"

After my shower, Miss Dade took me to the intake sergeant and explained.

"Listen, this guy says he's gay and in the Aryans, and they're gonna give him a beat down."

"No, I'm not in the Aryans." I corrected her. "My cellie is."

The desk sergeant told me to take off my shirt and turn around. He appraised my two, completely harmless tattoos and delivered a verdict.

"He's no fucking Aryan."

This was going south real fast. I tried to avoid using my *you-idiotic-pricks* voice and stay calm.

"*No*, I'm not an Aryan. That's not what I said. I said I was gay, and my cellie's an Aryan and I think that he might do something ugly about it."

Miss Dade was a little embarrassed.

"I thought you said you were a gay Aryan. We've never had one of those."

"Right, well, I apologize, I was talking kind of fast, but no, I'm just a regular gay, and every day I get my HIV meds and Drifter is starting to get suspicious."

I didn't know if he really was, but it sounded like hard evidence.

The sergeant hesitated. I looked at him with pleading eyes. "I was only supposed to be here one night. It's been a week."

The sergeant checked his clipboard.

"Name and number?

"Olmsted. V-31179."

He scanned the first page, and the one behind it, then scanned both of them again carefully, before reluctantly turning to the third page. I had the distinct sense that I was not supposed to have been forgotten like that. I was a minimum-security first-time offender who had been parked for a week in a SDU run completely by prison gangs.

This was one of the moments in prison when sounding educated worked to my advantage. I seemed like a person who was fully capable of filing a huge lawsuit if something happened to me, and that prospect probably made him nervous. But I decided the smartest move was to allay that concern, 'cause I just wanted out of there.

"This overcrowding sure doesn't make your job easier, does it?"

"No, it sure doesn't."

Thank God. I had him on my side now.

He grabbed another clipboard and scanned it slowly. Then he looked up at Miss Dade.

"Bunk opened up in Birch. Why don't you take him now?"

He scribbled my new bunk address on a piece of paper and handed it to me.

"Thank you, Officer."

In my entire life, I have never meant those words so sincerely. On the way back, Miss Dade added some crucial information.

"Don't tell Drifter where you're moving, okay?"

"Why? What's wrong with Birch?"

"It's a protective custody dorm."

I guess it wasn't considered good form for your cellie to find out you'd told the guards that you feared for your life at his hands.

Turns out I needn't have worried. In a farcical twist, when I got back to the cell, Drifter had all of his things ready to go. It turned out that Rebel's cellie had been "rolled up," and Drifter was going to take his place.

He assumed Miss Dade was going to escort him up.

"I'll be coming back for you. Gotta transfer Olmsted first."

Drifter suddenly noticed I'd been gathering up my things.

"Where are *you* going?"

"Cedar," I lied. "I told you, I was only supposed to be here a night."

Drifter was clearly irritated. I think he'd been hoping to move for weeks, in order to become Rebel's lieutenant and cellie. I deprived him of the pleasure of pointedly leaving my gay ass behind at the mercy of whatever Aryan replaced him.

Of course, we both obeyed social convention and pretended to be bummed that our time together had been so brief. It flashed through my mind to ostentatiously check to see if all my poems were still present and accounted for, but I didn't want to delay by a millisecond getting out of there.

As Miss Dade ushered me out of the cell, she addressed Drifter.

"I'll be back to get you soon," she said, locking the cell door, "but we're not going anywhere if you don't have all that stuff washed off the walls."

Drifter stared out with the look of a shelter dog who's been told he had to clean up his own poop. I almost felt sorry for him.

When Miss Dade and I got out of the building, she couldn't help but notice my smile.

"Happy to get out of there?"

"You have no idea."

"Actually, I do. It's the way I feel every time I finish my shift."

I had to sit on a bench for a good hour before someone had the time to check me into Birch, and I kept thinking about what she said. No wonder she tolerated Drifter's artwork — it was something that made one day a little bit different from the one that came before.

True, she gets to leave that jail every day. But she also has to come back the next.

P.S. The story I'm sending under separate cover, *Fringe Benefits,* was inspired by the gray cement walls of the cell I shared with Drifter. Reminded me of our basement in Rockville.

Fringe Benefits

When we lived in Maryland, my father worked for various paper companies. He held a series of middle management jobs that, during the 1960s, a man without a college degree could land mostly just by virtue of being a well-spoken WASP. Never the corporate type, he would have been far better suited to being the principal of a middle school, for example. But if he lacked the sharp elbows required to jockey his way to the upper echelons of business, his bended elbow was perfectly made for the era of three-martini lunches. As an exceedingly nice guy who held his liquor fairly well, he was an attractive drinking companion. He wasn't into sports, but he knew to peruse the back pages of last night's newspaper for scores; he wasn't a womanizer, but could be trusted to keep quiet over a co-worker's indiscretions. Everybody liked Steve Olmsted.

Occasionally, he would take a business trip, and my mother would take advantage of his absence to dispense with the usual way of doing things. I now see that she probably hoped to recreate the clubhouse feeling that existed between her and us before we started grammar school. We could watch TV as we ate, usually the Dick Van Dyke Show or I Love Lucy. She would make a pitcher of very milky tea, and we would eat "crazy meals" marked by one big fun entrée like spaghetti. During the commercials, someone would ask, "Please don't pass the butter!" – then declare – Opposite Day!" (Only as an adult did I discover we hadn't made up this game.)

When my father was home, dinner was promptly at six. In the warm months, around 5:45 or so, my father would stand on our porch, letting out a long two-toned whistle that would pen-

etrate every far-flung nook and cranny in the neighborhood. We had five minutes to finish up whatever game we were playing, five minutes to run home, and five minutes to wash our hands and make sure we were wearing a clean shirt. I can't remember ever being late for dinner.

If traditions such as "no advertising on the table" (like milk cartons), and monogrammed napkin rings were a legacy of my father's upbringing, establishing a topic of conversation at the table was truly his own idea. He made sure that all of us had a chance to have our say. Otherwise, my brother Luke and I would dominate the proceedings — he being naturally bossy and me naturally talkative. My dad would try to sum up our various contributions or impose a theme of sorts. This worked fine in principle, but in practice his consumption of Zinfandel made him a weak Master of Ceremonies. More often than not, his illustrative anecdote would miss the very point he was trying to make, or his poorly constructed joke would land with a thud. We would feel embarrassed for him, me in particular. My mother would say, "Oh, Steve" wearily, then suggest we clear the table. We would gratefully comply.

A few times when my Dad was going into his raconteur manqué mode, I stumbled onto a one-liner that managed to make his misfire seem like a set-up for my joke. Not only would the tension be broken, but everyone would burst out laughing, and I would take pleasure in saving my father from appearing foolish. I began to dread his stories and unfunny jokes less as I became better and better at turning him into Ed McMahon to my Johnny Carson.

Had his alcoholism turned my father mean or violent, life would have been more difficult, but less confusing. None of us except my mother had yet connected the cocktails to what seemed like a corresponding drop in I.Q every evening. I simply recognized that my dad was the parent who never seemed to answer a direct question with a direct answer, and would be perfectly happy to help you with your math but could never spot an error in your work.

I knew that when a TV dad came back from a business trip, the children clamored to find out what he'd brought home for them. I also knew mine wasn't that kind of dad, but asked once anyway, just in case. Almost apologetically, he came up with one of those small little airplane bottles, empty of its bourbon. Nothing could have pleased me more.

Down in the basement, the younger four of us — Luke, Sandra, Erica and I — would play, "White Trash Family." The little airline bottle, filled with tea, was the perfect prop for Luke as the gruff, working class father. As we "ate," he would swill it down, pretending to get increasingly drunk and abusive. This was thrilling to us in the same way a scary movie might have been had we been allowed to watch one. Sandra expertly played the cowering wife, keeping her head down, waiting for the first inevitable faux swat of many. I would vainly try to fend off the brute, as little Erica pretended to eat her invisible cereal while looking on in horror that was only half-pretend. (My poor sister could never understand why we couldn't just play regular "house.")

Eventually, our pretend dysfunctional family evolved into a tableau for a bona fide haunted house. We nailed some two-by-fours across the underside of the steps, fashioning an enclosure in which I played a humped creature kept at bay by my brother, as he cracked a bullwhip against the concrete floor of the basement. Doubling as guide, Luke would greet the neighborhood kids at the basement door in a cape, a flashlight in his face providing ghoulish illumination. He would then take the wide-eyed guests along a path to a table where my sister Sandra, dressed as a crone, would offer them "eyes for sale "— bloody marbles in ketchup-stained cotton. Erica would be hidden under the table, poking at their little legs with something wet. Then came my animal shrieks from under the stairs, which would propel them to the exit going up to the garage and back into the driveway and street. Not bad for five cents, but since we wanted repeat business, we were always coming up with new features.

One day Luke and I took one of Erica's old dolls, put a noose on her, and dangled her over a water pipe that threaded its way across the ceiling. I had the bright idea to light her hair on fire, a reckless suggestion for a goody-two-shoes like me, probably born from an intense desire to impress my older brother. I remember my shock when he agreed we should try it, as the de rigueur reaction to any idea generated by me was a scowl. Matches were taken from the ashtray where my father rested his pipe, and an attempt was made to drop the doll into an empty toy chest with her hair on fire.

We hadn't counted on the flame-retardant nature of the doll's nylon hair, so all we managed was some minor singeing, to my secret relief. (I liked the idea of being "bad" far more than actually being bad.) But the word "singe" evoked something else, another phrase that danced at the edge of my tongue. I had overheard it when my parents were discussing the merits of a job offer my father was considering.

Luke released the rope, and chest slammed shut on that poor doll. The moment called for some sort of caption, a signature, le mot juste. And suddenly the adult phrase I had recently learned popped into my head. I waited a full second, then delivered it in my best Vincent Price.

"Fringe benefits..."

Perhaps this is only mildly amusing in retrospect, but I can say without a doubt that at the time, it killed. Even my brother, who usually went out of his way to avoid acknowledging my jokes, could not stop laughing. More importantly, neither could I. I felt the rush of being intentionally witty; the payoff of constantly juxtaposing different combinations of words and ideas against each other and then delivering the result at precisely the right moment.

Being funny was my first addiction.

In 1968, my father started working at the West Virginia Pulp & Paper Company. We loved calling him at work. The word "pulp" was just plain fun to say, and then there was the alliteration when it was followed by "paper." Those poor receptionists had to say the whole mouthful every time, no doubt amused at the paroxysms of giggles this provoked when we heard, "West Virginia Pulp & Paper Company; how may I direct your call?"

In 1969, the company renamed itself Westvaco, and transferred my father to New York. The next year we moved to Mount Vernon, the first stop on an easy commute for my dad to Grand Central Station. The house was a perfectly lovely Tudor on a leafy street, but the town itself was far more Bronx than Bronxville, and our new schools were full of abrasive kids of every ethnicity speaking in a very scary accent.

The basement of our new home was serviceably dank and grey, but we felt no need to replicate our haunted house. The mean streets of New Yawk were plenty full of terrors, thank you very much.

Familiar Face

Birch Hall is actually a former day room into which 50 or so bunk beds have been crammed quite close to each other. There is a TV in one corner; in the opposite corner are the bathrooms and showers, which are more like drains in the floor surrounded by curtains. The nicest word for all of this might be *makeshift*.

I'm in the back, on a top bunk, of course. When I arrived from Sycamore two days ago, my bunkie was working in the kitchen, so I just settled in and looked around. Like County, it is relatively unsegregated. I would say about one-third of the inmates are transgender or openly gay, another third are straight but older, and some of us could qualify to be here either on the grounds of age or sexual orientation. The other third are informants and pedophiles of all ages. Even though that conjures up images of gargoyles and rats, I'll take them any day over an Aryan skinhead. There are also at least two guys in wheelchairs, and no doubt a few with serious health issues that are not readily apparent.

While it was fresh in my mind, I immediately started to write down everything about the week I'd just endured, and halfway through I noticed that the guy on the lower bunk to my right — who had been taking a nap — was awake and blinking in my direction. When he sat up, we realized that we recognized each other.

"Mark?"

"Danny?"

This was like running into Whisper at Delano, but even better! (I'm starting to believe in guardian angels. Maybe Luke is watching out for me.)

I can't remember if I mentioned Danny back in my letters

from County, but he was one of the good-looking Latin boys whom Larry managed to keep on hand with a steady flow of meth and money. Oh, God, that sounds sordid, but it wasn't. Danny wasn't in love with Larry, but he didn't pretend to be, either, and you never got the feeling he didn't want to be there. Once you got past the wizened Okie twang, Larry was easy to like. Very generous, but never wielded his money like a weapon.

Danny was perfectly happy to see me, but a little surprised at how glad I was to see him. Then I explained that I'd just come from, "Stickamore" and he immediately understood. He actually knew Rebel from Hemet. "He had a big meth lab out in the desert. Larry bought from him a few times — we even partied together once." I told him the blow job joke that got me so nervous. Danny got a big kick out of that. "He got that one from personal experience, believe me."

Larry had once told me Danny's story. When he was 14, his mother, to whom he was extremely close, was diagnosed with ovarian cancer. A good student before then, he started to cut class to stay home to take care of her. (I don't think his Dad was ever in the picture.) When his mom died, he dropped out for good and went to live with his grandparents. They didn't really know what to do with this clearly gay, grief-stricken kid who started to stay out every night, hustling for money and drugs. Run-ins with the law ensued, and at least one stint in prison before this one.

Danny himself had told me that Larry offered the greatest stability he'd found in years. Larry gave Danny a place to stay and, surprisingly enough, made no demands on him sexually. Larry actually wanted Danny to get his GED and go to college, but meth, of course, screws up everything.

Danny told me his sentence was much shorter than it would have been because Larry had paid for a decent lawyer. I know the cops found lots of meth in their apartment. Danny got the same length term that I received — 16 months. (Larry got twice that.)

Not that Danny is pining away for him. He doesn't blame

Larry for anything that happened, but he's "sure as shit" not picking up where they left off.

"I can't go back to that life," he told me.

"Me neither," I agreed.

And then, a second later, we said exactly the same thing in unison:

" 'Cause *nothing* is worth this shit."

Blink of an Eye

Thank God Danny was here to give me the rundown on the rules governing the bathroom. Since we only have five commodes here, there are two designated "pissers" and two designated "shitters." It is a real no-no to piss in a shitter or vice-versa. The fifth one is an emergency back-up if two of the sit-down commodes are already in use, but you try to avoid that. Of course, all of this concern for hygiene doesn't translate to anyone wanting to actually clean the bathrooms, so they bribe volunteers by giving them control over the TV. In fact, you can always tell that some kind of playoff game is going to be on when the straight guys are suspiciously willing to grab a mop in the morning.

Although this is worlds better than Sycamore, the dorm format makes it much harder to avoid the assholes, who, being assholes, have no idea they are assholes. I pretty much put up with their attempts to socialize, as I've learned by now that you never know when you might end up needing an unexpected ally. But after five minutes of the most inane conversation, I'll gamely point out that I need to finish the letter I'm writing to get it in the day's mail, to which they inevitably respond, "But, dude, you're always writing letters!"

We don't have library privileges here, but there are 20-some paperbacks floating around, and I got my hands on Jean Auel's *Clan of the Cave Bear.* I completely missed it back in the '70s, but am glad I did so that I could enjoy it fresh now. She's such a good storyteller, and I've already spent hours submerging myself in the pre-historic world she creates. I also have my eye on a thick Pat Conroy I spotted, but the guy who's reading it wants three soups to hand it over when he's finished. Considering that these books belong to the whole dorm, I just frowned and walked away.

My bunkie's name is Dick. He's 58, a former investment banker and the father of three grown kids. He's diabetic and suffers from poor circulation in his legs. Although he's not gay, every night he "hires" one of the boys who doesn't have money on his books to massage his feet. He works in the kitchen, and mostly pays them in food he smuggles out. (Because of his age, I think he'll do most of his time here, which is why he has a job.)

Birch is a place for prisoners who would be in danger elsewhere, including informants. For this reason, people tend to shade the stories of how they got here even more than usual — just in case you're a plant. That's why I'm not entirely sure of the veracity of Dick's story. It feels a bit like an account he learned to retell exactly the same way to a judge and a jury as part of a very specific legal strategy.

The short version — there was a company picnic, a softball game, and too much beer consumed. One of Dick's sons got into a fight over a bad call, and an alarmed Dick swung a baseball bat at the aggressor, intending to hit him in the leg. However, due to a terrible case of momentary lost footing, the bat slammed into the side of the victim's head.

Dick, horrified, called an ambulance; then fled the state to a second home, anxiously waiting to find out if he'd killed the guy. Thank God, the brain swelling went down and the poor man recovered. Dick returned from Arizona and turned himself in. He negotiated his way to a five-year sentence — aggravated assault and battery — but he'll have to serve 80% of it.

It doesn't seem like he could be lying about something that so many people witnessed, but my gut tells me that he's actually taking the fall for one of his sons, who sounds like a hotheaded alcoholic always getting into trouble. And, of course, Dick feels worst of all of for his wife, who was looking forward to a plush retirement and suddenly has to come visit her husband behind bars.

After he told me the story, everything I thought to say seemed like a hopelessly leaden platitude. Dick, however, knew exactly what to say, and I realized it would apply whether he had almost killed a man or actually taken the blame for a son who had.

"The moral of the story, my friend, is that your life can totally change in a split-second." He snapped his fingers. "Like that."

The truth of his words lay there like an 800-pound dead gorilla, and it felt like we were both about to descend into a suicidal depression. I decided to lighten things up.

"You know what's worse, Dick? Sometimes things can change gradually, over a 10-to-15 year period."

For the longest second, I thought I'd completely overthought a punch-line, but then he got it and let out a deep, booming laugh that literally shook the room.

Leave Some for Us

On Monday there was no mail because of the three-day July 4th weekend, but it did make me fairly optimistic that I would get more than usual today. I wasn't prepared, however, to break a record.

The mail is sorted by bunk number. I am BD-15, at the end of a stretch of the first 14 bunks. Stokes, who is one of the nicest guards, walked down the row, handing out a letter here and a letter there, maybe one for every other inmate. It's always bittersweet to watch this because some guys never get a stick of mail, and you know they're not going to get mail, and they know it, too. Yet no matter how much they pretend not to be paying attention, you know they have an ear cocked when Stokes walks by, and they experience a split-second of involuntary hope, inevitably dashed. I've observed that one guy always goes to the bathroom during mail call; I think this is why.

I'm well aware that the guys notice how much mail I receive. I actually overheard Vinnie and Nubia (a funny New Yorker and a regal ex-dancer) try to make a bet that some day soon I wouldn't receive a single letter. Neither would take the bet.

This afternoon, Stokes arrived at my bunk, repeating my name each time he tossed a letter to me on the bunk. "Olmsted... Olmsted... Olmsted... Olmsted... Olmsted... Olmsted..." I thought he was finished, but last came a large manila envelope, and he added — with a slight trace of sarcasm, "...and *Olmsted.*"

Someone yelled out, "Damn, dude, leave some for us!" Even though he said it in jest, there was an edge to it, as if on some level he believed that the more mail I receive, the less everybody else does. And there was another subtext, one that I was perhaps making up in my head, but couldn't help but feel nonetheless. *"You pathetic motherfucker! You've got so many people who love you that much! You think if I had that many people who loved me that my sorry ass would be in in prison?"*

"No," I answered in my head. *"But I am a man of singular talent, and found a way to fuck up in spite of all that love. And miraculously enough, their love has remained unflagging and unconditional, and I promise you, I don't take any of it for granted."*

This batch of love was from Mireille, Henri, Claudine, Mom and Francoise, Andrea and Sandra, twice — a regular letter and then the big envelope. And that big envelope was what stopped the envy of the onlookers from curdling into antipathy, because of the treasures inside of it.

The stationery was genius! Sandra must have chosen something from every drawer in what has to be Albuquerque's only specialty paper store. It seemed like everybody in the dorm was watching me pull out what was inside, and I attracted a veritable swarm as soon as Stokes finished his rounds.

I had something for everybody. In addition to the array of specialty stationery, there were several colored pencils and a sheet of Disney character stamps. These were particularly thrilling for Winston, who is always trying to hustle the guys to pay him to do their portraits to send home. I've never seen one agree to it, but immediately one of the dads said if Winston did "a real good Little Mermaid," one that he could send home to his four-year-old, he'd give him five soups. I told Winston I'd loan him the colored pencils to do it, but only if he gave me Pat Conroy's *Beach Music.* He handed it over immediately! (Winston was the guy who wanted three soups for it last week. He looks menacing but I think he's actually a puppy dog.)

Whatever resentment was felt about my hogging of the incoming mail totally evaporated. Once again "Mark's sister" made Mark a very popular guy. (I'm not going to embarrass her by getting too sentimental, but let's just say that the phrase "immense gratitude" doesn't begin to cut it.)

P.S. Stokes is the one who told me I broke a record. "I've been working here nine years, and I swear I never saw anybody get more than five pieces of mail in one day."

Starr Power

Each week we have clothing/linen exchange, where we turn in most everything we have for new or laundered material. I say "most," because inmates always hold back what they can. But since they have to turn something in to get something back, the strategy is to rip a sheet in two, turning half in and keeping the other half — which they then rip up further to fashion cords from which to hang laundry or makeshift curtains. They also keep extra blankets, which are tightly rolled and tied, and then placed sideways and used as stools (picture sitting on a can). Every few weeks, the C.O.'s clear everyone out of the dorm and make us wait in the dining room while they purge our bunks of all this extra contraband. Then the game starts anew.

Most of the clothing is hopelessly oversized, so if you're not one for the baggy-pants look (the racial divide is stark on this matter), you tend to hold onto a pair that fits, even if that means washing it yourself.

I've only seen one inmate whose chief problem is finding a uniform that's large *enough*. Starr is 6'6", and I have to say that it's a cruel God who would give basketball genes to an effeminate, gender-questioning kid from a poor, black family. Not surprisingly, Starr (for whom I will use the pronoun "she" henceforth) has developed a bit of an attitude as a survival tool. Unfortunately, she is so fearful of being the butt of a joke that she tends to strike first, and often her prickly wit ends up losing her far more friends than it wins.

The only person who refuses to react to her preemptive trash-talk is "Doc," a 50ish trans inmate (you wouldn't know it but for a pair of small but noticeable breasts) who has the sort of knowing attitude of an older black woman in the movies — a bootlegger or a madam, perhaps, with bifocals perched on her nose and a cigarette perpetually dangling from her lip. (Well, she would, if we could smoke here.) Her heavy-lidded eyes speak of someone who has seen it all and is impressed by nothing. Except, perhaps, Starr's crackerjack skills at pinochle, a game that happens to be Doc's one absolute passion. They play for hours, with verve and emphasis, trading barbs that are often quite funny. (These tend to be of the "you-had-to be-there" variety, so I won't try to replicate them.)

Since they are both broke, they play for who will do the other's laundry. But they don't really hold each other to it. If one gets started with a bucket and a bar of soap, the other will at least rinse out the garment and hang it on a clothesline made from one of the aforementioned contraband sheets.

During these sessions, they are no longer Doc and Starr, but "Quida" and "Shaquida," two characters meant to be tough girls from back in the 'hood, I think. What really happens, though, is that they tend to morph into versions of their church-lady mothers — from "mothafucka" to "lawdie, lawdie" in less than five minutes, I swear.

The other day Stokes had arranged for the local R&B radio station to be piped in through the sound system during his Saturday shift. Etta James' classic *At Last* came on, and Doc and Starr took a break from their Quida-ing to enjoy the music. Suddenly, Doc stopped wringing out a pair of pants, because she noticed that the voice she was hearing along with Etta's was Starr's, and it was pretty good.

I observed this from across the room, and went over for a closer look. Sure enough, Starr's pipes were impressive, and by the last stanza, she was giving a performance, her eyes closed and her posture straightening unapologetically to her full height. With a final flourish, she extended that long arm upwards and flicked her hand dramatically on the last note. A few of us were gathered around at this point, and we gave her a round of applause.

Doc was the first to speak:

"Damn, Shaquida, you can sing!"

Starr blushed, suddenly embarrassed by the attention. Then her lips started to quiver, and she turned away from us and covered her face, so we would not see her cry.

Cage Fight

Even though I haven't written much about Danny, he's made my stay at Birch so much better in all kinds of little ways. For example, a few days after I arrived here, I got it in my head to create a new hybrid art form named "Taroetry." (I'm sure someone's already thought of it, but I don't have Google to find out, so let's just say I invented it.) I cut up the poems Sandra had sent me in Sycamore into quarters, and created a "deck." I then numbered each one in Romanian (a list Thumper had made for me) to make them more exotic, and finally wrote notes on the back of each that suggested predictive meanings based on the words of the poem on the other side.

See? "Tarot" plus "Poetry" = "Taroetry."

Danny was the guinea pig for my first reading, which was, of course, entirely improvised on my part. But he was extremely attentive, and listened as if I was a talented seer. His kind reaction notwithstanding, I don't think fortunetelling will become a sideline. It was one of those ideas that seem brilliant on paper but not so much in practice.

He next impressed me playing softball. He has a naturally athletic body and a fantastic swing that just *blammed* the ball over left field. The straight boys did not expect that from one of us, let me tell you.

One of them is a consummate dickwad who gets on everybody's nerves. His name is Albert, and he wants to be called "Al" but it just doesn't stick, because he's not cool enough to have a one-syllable name.

Maybe "dickwad" is a little harsh, but he's *so* annoying. Rumor has it that he's a J-Cat — someone with a mental health diagnosis. In any case, he's got a nasty temper that flares up just as you're starting to feel sorry for him. The other day, trying to be "one of the guys," he used the word "fag," and Danny went ballistic on him. He pulled his hand back in a fist and was ready to clock Albert, who lost all semblance of bravado in a whimpering millisecond.

In all these many years of being a proud gay man, I have never seen one of us actually ready to come to blows in defense of our collective honor. To witness it here, in a place where homosexuality is unrelentingly equated with passivity, was particularly thrilling.

This eloge to Danny has been prompted by his departure this morning to Del Norte, which is on the other side of the prison from where I'm headed, Redwood Hall (after two weeks or so in Cedar, for "orientation.") I'll probably be gone by the end of the week.

Danny clearly felt touched that I was bummed that we weren't headed to the same place. He's the kind of guy who never seems to realize how well-liked he is. I get the feeling he hasn't let many people get close to him since his mother died, a defense mechanism that meth made fairly easy to maintain.

I won't be leaving a moment too soon, frankly, as there are a few inmates with whom I really am losing patience. One of them is talkative black guy with a New Orleans accent named Cage. (Short for "Cajun," I think.) Because he's in a wheelchair, I cut him a lot of slack, and then I realized how he uses his disability to manipulate everyone. He even proudly described all of the crimes he's gotten away with which would have gotten anyone else sent to prison long before. He's a little vague about what line he finally crossed, but Doc is under the impression that he shot someone.

Cage's most annoying habit is to tickle the feet of men lying on their bunks, reading or napping. This sounds harmless enough, but he only chooses inmates he thinks would never hit someone in a wheelchair. The first time he did it to me, I rolled my eyes. The second time I was genuinely pissed, as I had just dozed off. I reacted sharply.

"You do that again and you will regret it, Cage."

Today he did it again, and I was in no mood, because Danny had just left. I jumped off my bunk as he sped away as fast as his wheels could take him. I caught up with him right next to his bunk, cornering him against the wall. Imitating Danny, I pulled back my fist like a cocked bow, and came very close to releasing it. But Cage put his hands up and cried out, "I'm sorry, I'm sorry, I promise, I won't do it again!" I decided to hold my fist there for another five seconds, and then, very slowly brought it to my side. I said nothing, and walked back to my bunk.

It may seem like an over-reaction, but it will be well worth getting an undisturbed nap. More importantly, he'll think twice about inflicting one of his meandering, pointless anecdotes on me.

I'd rather he steal my food than my time, any day.

Standing on my Head

I have just moved into Cedar Hall, where I'll spend the next couple of weeks in "orientation" — which feels a lot more like quarantine. We wear orange and aren't allowed to mix with the general population, although we can see them, in their blue uniforms, through our fenced-in courtyard. If someone painted us from afar, particularly at dusk, it would actually make a lovely tableau.

The dorm consists of four wings (A, B, C and D) radiating from a central guard booth, and it feels much less "prisoney" than anywhere I've been so far. We have windows and a giant fan at the end of each corridor to keep us cool. Ah, minimum security, at last.

I had to leave behind the book I was reading, but do have the PEN Journal Sandra sent me, so I've delved happily into several erudite literary articles, including one by a professor I used to work with at NYU. I feel like I am conducting graduate seminar in my head, with myself as the sole participant.

It's quite a contrast to the conversational loop going on around me — what joint they came from, who they did time with, when we can fill out our canteen orders, blah, blah, blah. Prison, prison, prison! You'd never know there was a national election campaign going on, for example. I wouldn't be surprised if I was the only person in here who has ever voted.

I remember making a similar observation when I was a dealer. Nearly every conversation seemed to be about drugs — how good the shit was, who you last got high with, and where to go for more. And then just when it dawned on you that perhaps you were being deadly boring, you'd get high and suddenly everyone seemed plenty interesting.

I've started to think about the possibility of getting a Master's degree when I get out. I should have gone for it while I was working at NYU (the tuition would have been free), but persuaded myself that I didn't want to get locked into teaching French and risk never becoming a screenwriter. The bullshit we feed ourselves at 25! Being a teacher looks pretty damn good to me right about now. I wonder if I could put this experience on my resume if I agreed to work in a *really* bad neighborhood.

At least I had the self-discipline back then to come into the office every Saturday morning to knock out my first screenplay. I worked on it for the better part of a year, using the one computer shared by the entire French Department and a software program called "Spellbinder." It never crossed my mind that I would ever write on anything other than a PC. But here I am, 20 years later, writing more than ever with nothing but a pen and paper.

Well, if it was good enough for Flaubert, it's good enough for me.

One of the requirements of "orientation" is taking the TABE (Test of Basic Education Skills). In principle, it allows inmates to be placed at the right level in classes that will help them earn a GED. Unfortunately, those courses have almost entirely gone on the chopping block since "rehabilitation" became code for "soft on crime" and the prison/industrial complex took over the national justice system. Somehow, this one pointless test survived the cuts. I guess the California Bureau of Corrections wants data at the ready just in case the pendulum swings back to prison reform. They could save a shitload of money if they'd just asked Victor Hugo his opinion. In 1850, he wrote, "Open a school and you close a prison." (I remember that from a paper I wrote at Stony Brook way back in 1977.)

Given the fact that these test results probably rot away in file cabinets, I don't understand why the test is mandatory, but it is.

I only discovered this when Cutter, who bunks across from me, refused to take it. It's hard not to notice Cutter, who looks like a young Billy Dee Williams and has a silky-smooth voice to match. I can easily believe that he's as successful a pimp as he says he is, and in spite of knowing how he makes his living, I can't manage to dislike him.

Racial politics being thick when you arrive anywhere in the system, I haven't had a direct conversation with Cutter, but the way he tells a story indicates that he's not just street-smart, but smart-smart. At least smart enough to realize that he could make a lot more money stealing cars and running girls than by completing high school.

He has been in prison three times. While you might think that doesn't seem so smart, it merely indicates how difficult it is to escape the system once you're in it. The only job available to a high school dropout with a record is minimum wage, so why wouldn't someone return to a life of fast cash and plenty of it? By the time guys like Cutter are in their '20s, they usually have a few children as well, but they often won't visit the kids if they can't show up with gifts and money. That's their definition of being a good father. I asked one of these guys why he didn't just drop by occasionally to read his son a bedtime story.

"Oh, c'mon, man," he answered, shaking his head as if I knew damn well he'd look like a fool doing such a thing.

Cutter was summoned to the warden's office for refusing to show up for the test, and when he returned, I heard his bunkie ask what happened.

"I ain't taking the test again, that's what happened."

"That's it? They ain't penalizing you?"

"I didn't say that! They gave me 67 extra days."

"Oh, shit, man, that's harsh!"

Cutter brushed it off.

"I can do two months standing on my head."

"It's just a test, man!"

"Fuck their damn test. I ain't taking it again."

Cutter had evidently not done well the last two times he'd taken the TABE, and found it deeply humiliating to be told the test scores indicated he wasn't as smart as he damn well knew he was. He had a thriving business to prove it, after all.

"I had six females working for me!" he explained. "And I didn't even have to lay a hand on them to keep them in line. They were begging to come work for me, 'cause I treated them right! Shit, one of my females got sick, and I'd take care of her myself!"

He changed his shirt, revealing a sinewy torso that further blinded me to his faults.

"So I can't do motherfucking geometry! Who gives a shit? I can count money, and I was pulling in 300K a year, tax-free! Hell, I bought a condo *for cash!*"

I took all of this with a grain of salt, of course, particularly the part about granting sick days and personal nursing care to his staff. But clearly he saw himself as way too successful an entrepreneur to be, and I quote, "in a class full of remedial niggas!"

Wherever the truth lay, I quietly reeled at the idea that anyone would choose to be here even one extra day rather than take a test. Try as I might, I just couldn't understand it.

Hazardous to Your Health

Spanky, the white shotcaller here, called a meeting of the Woods in the day room. Once we crowded in, he proceeded to read from a newspaper article which he claimed had appeared in a recent issue of the *L.A. Times.* It concerned a recent study attesting to the presence of antibodies to HIV in saliva. I'm pretty certain that the topic of the article was not HIV transmissibility, but rather how oral HIV tests work. Far be it for me, however, to get in the path of an ignorance train barreling full speed down the tracks.

After sharing these informative excerpts, Spanky (who has a tattoo of the TV character on his neck) held forth with the acuity and wit to which I have become accustomed in this elite gentlemen's club. A brief summation, "I don't care what anybody says, you <u>can</u> get this shit by smoking or drinking 'after' someone who's HIV-positive!" He swaggered in place as he talked, gathering steam while laying down the law. "I don't want to see ANY-BODY who's HIV-positive sharing anything with anybody else. And as far as I'm concerned, it's on YOU to let anybody know! And if you don't, and I find out later that you are, I'll fucking kick your ass!"

My first thought was that it was unenforceable paranoid bullshit, but he wasn't finished.

"So I want everyone who's gay or bisexual to raise their hand."

The moment was so unexpected that I was completely panicked. Even though his demand didn't relate to me personally, that's what it felt like in my gut. After all, Drifter had told me that inmates working in the warden's office routinely leaked the contents of one's "jacket" (the file kept on each of us) to the gang heads of each of the races. That's why Rebel might easily have known about my status back in Sycamore.

The rest of my calculus was instinctive. Better to out myself and get credit for honesty (and bravery, frankly), than later be accused of attempted murder because someone asked if he could eat the rest of my apple and I let him. And perhaps I was inspired by Danny's assertion of gay pride back at Birch.

What the fuck. I raised my hand.

Tentatively, another hand followed mine. Two out of 50 or so men in the room wasn't half-bad, considering where we were.

I don't think Spanky had expected anyone to respond at all.

"All right, then!" he sputtered out. "Don't eat or smoke after these guys!"

He finished up with the requisite, "Woodpile!" callout, which was the signal for everybody to leave. Knowing how many eyes were on me, I tried not to look too obviously in the direction of the other confessee, whose face had been blocked from view when his hand went up.

The curiosity didn't seem to be mutual, however. Everyone in that area of the room was already clearing out, and I saw only backs.

I had no idea who my potential ally in here might be.

Lefty and Righty

On the way out of the day room after the meeting, I saw Spanky hand the newspaper clipping to a guard, or should I say, "back to a guard," as their exchange definitely had a well-rehearsed quality to it. Spanky is shotcaller here because he is one of the few inmates who actually lives in Cedar — it makes sense that he might have a close relationship with one of the guards here. But he doubtfully has access to a newspaper, so almost certainly the C.O. is the one who brought the article to his attention.

I expect ignorance from inmates — I'm well used to it. And I don't expect a prison guard to have a background in public health. But catering to an irrational fear of fatal contagion is an inexcusable form of incitement, as it could actually put someone like me in physical danger.

I haven't had a look at this clown's badge yet, so I'll call him Sargent Clavin, inspired by Cliff on *Cheers,* the know-it-all postman who can't keep his mouth shut about practically any topic under the sun. Even from afar, this Clavin has the vibe of a self-imagined "mentor" who thinks he is teaching wayward young men like Spanky a few valuable life lessons.

The whole thing got me royally pissed off. Luckily Lefty was at our bunk, and his reaction to the whole day-room incident buoyed me. He called it "complete crap."

I haven't introduced Lefty. He's my new bunkie, and has that nickname because his right hand is shriveled from palsy. That made it a little bit harder for him to swing up on the top bunk, so even though I got here before he did, I gave him the bottom bunk. At 23, he's from a generation that tends not to give a shit whether someone's gay, but his disability has definitely made him sensitive to anyone being marginalized. (So my good bunkie kar-

139

ma remains intact!)

I felt comfortable asking him what he was in for, so here's the backstory. Lefty grew up in the high desert on his dad's ranch with his older brother, currently in Afghanistan. When he was around 14, his mother died.

"What happened?" I asked.

"Lead poisoning," he answered. My first thought was that they lived next to a toxic waste dump or something, but he followed it up with a gesture of a gun to the head, and I realized he was referring to the bullet with which she shot herself. I listened for any elaboration as to why she committed suicide, but he didn't offer one, and I wasn't going to ask. (In my mind's eye, his mother blamed herself for his birth defect, perhaps because of drinking while she was pregnant. Just a guess, though.)

Lefty changed the subject to his one abiding passion — cars. He loves working on them, fixing them, driving them. I didn't have much to offer on the subject except that I thought my Aunt Nancy's 1959 Rambler was incredibly cool when I was a kid, but if there was one classic chassis to mention, that was it, as Lefty loves tail fins from the '50s and '60s.

He also loves booze, and evidently got accustomed to thinking it was no big deal to joyride drunk in the desert. It took years before he was pulled over, and then they let him off with a warning "because they felt sorry for me." Eventually that stopped working, and he was arrested. And arrested. And arrested. After a half-dozen sentences to probation and AA meetings, the judge finally had enough and sent him here.

I asked Lefty if he'd noticed who else raised their hand in the room during the meeting.

"You don't know?" he asked.

"No, his face was blocked."

"Of all the faces not to see..." Lefty smiled. "It was the chin guy."

I instantly knew whom he was talking about.

Blue Collins is his name, no doubt because of his startling azure eyes, a trait you are grateful to focus on because he also has a jaw that is either deformed or dislocated or both. It literally swings far over to the right of his face, as if it was stuck in a freeze-frame photo taken during a boxing match. (To be honest, I think Lefty likes that there is somebody else in the dorm who gets more stares than he does.)

I know Blue's name because he bunks at the end of our wing, and I met him while he was snorting a Wellbutrin with Jaime, a kid I used to know at County. (As a Latino, Jaime hadn't been in the meeting of the whites, so was not there to identify as a gay person.) Given this new information, I realized in retrospect that the drug-sharing was probably part of Blue's courtship of Jaime.

Aside from the chin, Blue looks like an Olympic skier — tall, blond, V-shaped torso. For a body like that, I could personally look past the unfortunate jaw-line, but I am definitely the wrong age and ethnicity. Jaime, for his part, doesn't seem at all sure he likes the attention.

Ill-Considered

Miss. Reid is a no-nonsense African-American guard, around 50, who's worked exclusively in Cedar Hall for years. As she does her rounds, she often has conversations with inmates she recognizes from earlier terms. She says things like, "See, I told you you'd be back," which sounds mean, but they don't mind because at least she remembers them, and it makes them feel important.

And while Miss Reid strikes a don't-mess-with-me pose, she also lets a personal side shine though. For example, she has quite a collection of wigs, and she references them freely. An inmate will call out, "You look nice today, Miss Reid!" and she'll say something back like, "Damn right I do. I've been holding back on y'all, but I'm lettin' loose today!" She also tolerates a dorm cat. The way it rubs up against her leads me to believe she's the one feeding it.

I was able to call my sister this morning because Jaime gave me his phone time in exchange for my help cleaning the bathroom. While we mopped, I asked if he'd heard any of Blue's story — by which I meant, of course, if he knew what had happened to that jaw.

Jaime shook his head.

"I just know that he's coming from a Level II." (Medium Security.) "Did six and a half years there, and they're letting him transfer here to finish out his sentence."

Jaime probably didn't ask Blue what he was in here for because he didn't want to know. Sometimes people here will take you hostage with their stories. They'll tell you a secret about themselves, and then point to it as evidence of their intimacy with you.

We assumed that he'd probably done something violent, which most likely explained his Picasso-esque profile. On the other hand, he must have done spotless time to get knocked down a security level to finish out his sentence, so perhaps while behind bars, he'd shed an earlier persona. He wouldn't be the first person to be changed by prison in a good way.

As Jaime and I exited the bathroom together, we were laughing about something or another, and I spied Blue leaning against the wall opposite us, right against the guard's booth.

"Jeez," muttered Jaime.

Admittedly, Blue's gaze seemed a tad vulturine, but publically sporting an infatuation in prison struck me as brave more than anything else. Besides, Miss Reid had clearly taken notice through the glass partition of the office, and I knew that Jaime was one of her favorite porters.

I thanked Jaime again for the phone time and headed back to my bunk, thinking how ironic it was that all of these walls certainly didn't do much to teach boundaries.

I couldn't have been less prepared to hear Blue's voice erupting volcanically in the hallway I'd just left.

"Fuck with me, and I'll kill you bitch! And your cat, too!!"

In the space of a minute, Blue had gone from sulker to stalker to screamer; accusing Jaime of some imagined infidelity and then blowing up at Miss Reid when she told him to back off. The really odd thing was how instantaneously he realized he'd fucked up, apologizing with such dizzying speed that his explosion seemed like the split-second flare of a flame-thrower. He barely averted getting tased by Sargent Clavin, who was probably disappointed when Miss. Reid signaled to him not to bother.

After his vituperative threat, her *sang-froid* astounded me, actually.

"You know I'm going to have to roll you up for this, right, Mr. Collins?" she asked.

He nodded shamefacedly, turning around with his wrists behind him, offered for cuffing. Six and a half years of good behavior up in smoke in a moment of insanely misplaced jealousy. As he was led away, he glanced up at Jaime, as if somehow he could at least be granted pardon from him, if no one else.

It was all very *Hunchback of Notre Dame.*

When I got back to D-wing, I saw that Sargent Clavin had already dispatched Spanky and his little gang to clear out Blue's locker. It reminded me of piranhas picking a carcass clean. All of his letters and paperwork went in one box, while Spanky handed more desirable items to his confederates. Some toothpaste here, a box of crackers there. The spoils of war.

On his way back, Spanky noticed me watching, and stopped at my bunk. I was afraid that he was going to tell me to my mind own business, but instead he reached into the box, and held a book out to me.

"Here. You're always reading."

There was nothing hostile in his tone. I think it was his way of apologizing for putting me on the spot yesterday.

The book was a text entitled *The Indo-Europeans,* fat and heavy, right up my alley. As I leafed through it, I saw that Blue had used a photo as a place marker. There he was, about 17, standing at the edge of a lake in a bathing suit. His smile was as light and airy as the summer breeze that caught his blond hair, and his jawline was as perfect as can be.

He was one of the most beautiful men I'd ever seen.

Rudy

This morning I went to the doctor to discuss the bizarre pain in my feet which I experience every morning walking from my bunk to the bathroom. Uncharacteristically, I did not bring a book with me, but this turned out to be a good thing.

First, let me say that there are nowhere as many beautiful men here as one might imagine from some of my entries. There are a fair number of well-built guys and some serious cuties, to be sure. But let's face it, as a gay man I notice them more. The rest are as unappetizing as you'd imagine. (A life of crime is not the healthiest lifestyle, and it definitely takes a toll.)

That said, Rudy is one of the hot beauties about whom my rhapsodizing is justified. A new arrival, he caught my eye immediately. Although I tried to be discreet in noticing him, he unexpectedly smiled at me as we crossed paths in the dorm. It wasn't a cruise, more like a signal that he didn't mind getting checked out. He's fairly well-tattooed but no skinhead, thank God. Today we found ourselves together in the waiting room at the doctor's office, and I took a risk, introducing myself and extending my hand. He wouldn't take it, but for the nicest reason.

"Oh, dude, I'm here for this wicked cold. I don't want to give you anything." Indeed, he was very congested. It didn't help that he smoked, which I discovered when he invited me outside and offered me a Marlboro. From a real pack.

This is not something you can buy from the commissary, which only sells cans of tobacco from which you roll your own. I couldn't help but ask how he got them, and he smiled.

"That's what they call 'proprietary information,' my friend. Let's just say you get to know people over ten years."

This surprised me, because I hadn't met anyone who such a

long sentence at Chino.

"Oh no, that's not one term, that's a lot of little ones."

I cocked my head just a little to the side, to let him know I was listening, in case he felt like talking. He took a long drag on his cigarette, and started talking.

"You know, it might sound like I'm an unholy fuck-up, and I am, but let me tell you one thing. I've spent way more time in here because of candy-ass parole violations, or extensions to my sentence from infractions committed in here, than for any crime I actually committed on the outside."

I asked him to backtrack a little. What kind of family did he come from?

"I was a foster kid for most of my life, and then was on the street at 18 with nowhere to go. So I start hustling, doing petty shit, just to have a place to sleep at night..."

"Hustling" is one of those words that can go either way. To a gay ear, it means having sex for money with men. To a straight ear, "hustling" refers to various illegal ways to make money. I was pretty sure Rudy meant it in the former sense.

"So I end up doing this and that, but nothing serious, and they put me in County for 90 days, and it was rough, man. I was this pretty young kid everyone wanted to take advantage of, so I became a really good fighter to defend myself. Then I'd be out for maybe six months before I'd sell some coke to an undercover cop, and boom, I was back — but this time in real prison. I had no money on my books, so I started to figure out how to smuggle in drugs and tobacco, just to survive, really."

He told me that he had "relationships" with guards who brought in cigarettes and they all made money. (Again, unclear what else this involved, exactly.) He worked out a lot, learned to box, got his G.E.D. But then he'd get out, have trouble finding a place to stay or a job, start hustling again, violate his parole, return to prison, get caught smuggling or fighting, get punished and so on. Lather, rinse, repeat.

He didn't relate this in a defeatist or resentful tone, but with matter-of-fact humor devoid of self-pity, and perhaps a bit of pride at always finding a way to survive. (I listened for any reference to a girlfriend, past or present, but there was none.)

I would have gladly continued my friendly interrogation, but he was called in to see the nurse.

I have wicked crush on him, of course, made worse by my savior complex. I want to go back in time and slap his biological drug-addict mom into getting sober instead of giving him away. I want to cure his one nice foster mother of the diabetes that killed her. ("She was a really sweet woman. Just couldn't stop eating, I swear.")

Back when he was still a teenager, Rudy basically had to choose between living on the street or behind these walls. What insanity! It would cost far less to send every foster kid to college than to send them here. In Rudy's case, it definitely would have paid off. He's a born salesman and raconteur. He would have made a great businessman.

On his way out, he winked at me.

A minute later, the nurse asked if seeing the doctor made me nervous.

"No. Not at all, why?"

" 'Cause your pulse is a little fast, honey."

P.S. It would seem I have plantar fasciitis. The doc says it's common among inmates who are wearing flapjacks and haven't been able to order sneakers yet, as we have very little support in our feet. I shall order some as soon as I can get my first package at Redwood.

Here

This afternoon we were all forced to sit on the ground during a "Yard Down" alert, and I found myself next to an affable older black guy named "Pharmer." Of course, I initially thought it was "Farmer," and wondered if that's what he used to do for a living. But he explained it was short for "Pharmaceuticals," because he has a little sideline selling pain relievers. In fact, he struck up a conversation with me because of my slight limp due to the plantar fasciitis, asking if perhaps if I needed to buy some Advil. I told him I got one for free at each Pill Call, and he ended up teaching me a little about why it was cheaper for some inmates to buy from him.

He explained that the five dollars deducted from someone's books for a doctor's visit (which was news to me) was two days' wages for an inmate making 31 cents an hour, and it made much more sense for someone with migraines, for example, to come to him instead of get "free" meds at Pill Call.

It's very easy to feel sorry for yourself in prison, but every time I start to go down that road, I have an encounter that reminds me that I am still extremely lucky compared to most of these guys. I hadn't even noticed the co-pay because my family deposits $200 a month in my account. Imagine what it must be like for some of these families (like Pharmer's) to have to choose between gas money to visit their loved one and putting money on his books so that he can buy some toothpaste or see a doctor? Imagine if I could never call my sister because she couldn't afford to accept the jacked-up rates they charge for collect calls from prison?

"Jesus," I noted to Pharmer. "You'd think poverty was punishment enough for being poor."

"You got that shit right!"

He reminds me a lot of Carmelo — remember the guy who gave me that *Vanity Fair* at Delano? The one with the wife he divorced and remarried twice? They could be brothers.

Back at the dorm we continued our conversation. (This sort of casual contact between races isn't frowned upon here nearly as much as at Delano.) We had a long conversation about the psychology of prisoners. Pharmer summed it up like this:

"There's a lot of angry people here. Most of them because they don't know who they are. They don't know who their daddy is, and a lot of them, they don't know who their momma is neither. I had this girl on the streets, her momma left her in the hospital when she was on crack, and this girl cried and cried in my arms and said to me, 'I don't even know who I am, I don't even know who I am.'"

I was so struck by what he said that this poem came out of me in one draft afterwards:

Here

Here's to all the babies
who get left in cribs alone
who cry for hours
the saddest of songs.
Here's to all the toddlers
who get slapped and snapped at,
instead of missed and kissed.
Here's to all the kids
in foster homes or juvies,
who end up in prison
or mental hospitals,
behind bars
or drinking at them.
Here's to all the people who don't know who they are,
who don't know how to say —

149

"I am in so much pain,"
except on Jerry Springer or Cops,
screaming at a uniform.
Here's to all the guards
who should be teaching,
to all the dealers,
who should be healing.
Here's to building schools
with walls that support hope
instead of enclose it.
Here's to a world
too full of jails,
of injured men
with tortured tales.
Here's to making here, there,
and then, there, a place farther away.
Here's to me, here's to you,
Here's to being heard.

The Goldilocks Zone

A few days ago, I explained that Spanky didn't want anyone eating or smoking "after" someone who is gay or bisexual, i.e., possibly HIV+. What I didn't make clear is the larger context of this rule. In prison culture, the original sin has always been for a white inmate to eat or smoke after a black inmate. This is still very much in force — you can get your ass kicked if you take a drag off the cigarette a black inmate offers you, for example. The blacks aren't as strict in the reverse direction, but they generally don't eat "after" white inmates either. (Latinos think like the whites on this issue.)

All three races agree, however, that no one should ever smoke or eat after a known gay person. Initially I thought this was AIDS-phobia, but after several conversations I now realize it runs way deeper. The issue is less about catching a disease than the idea of being psychologically tainted by contact with lips that have ever been wrapped around a penis. More fundamentally, if you're eating or smoking after someone who sucks cock, you are being passive (accepting a gift or favor) to someone passive, and you may be tagged with the whiff of weakness. Since being perceived as vulnerable is what everyone fears most in prison, it has a distressing logic to it.

Figuring this out doesn't change much, but it makes it easier not to take any shunning personally. It truly has nothing to do with me.

Yesterday afternoon, I was the recipient of an orange at Pill Call, as the MTA (Medical Tech Assistant) had a few left over after distributing them to the diabetics. I peeled the orange at my bunk but hadn't yet taken a bite, so I offered a portion to Magoo, my Latin neighbor. He responded to my offer by asking, "Hey, you're gay. right?" in a nasal voice that probably has something to do with how he got his nickname. I nodded affirmatively, thinking that everyone in earshot probably knew anyway, and I'd get points for being upfront.

"Well," said Magoo, "I don't eat after gays because who knows where your hands have just been."

This lame attempt at a joke landed with a thud, sounding far more hostile than it was meant to. And yet he didn't retract it, because he had been trying to show everybody he wasn't about to violate the rules about "eating after" gays. Even his bunkie, Cookie, thought he was out of line.

"Gee, dawg, what side of the bed did you get up on this morning?"

I just played it cool, withdrew the orange and started to break it into segments. If the moment was uncomfortable, that was going to have to fall on his shoulders, not mine.

That evening I had the good luck to get a second pillow from a guy I knew at Birch. (He's in a wheelchair, but faking his injury because he's suing the cops for beating him up.) As I placed the pillow on my bed, Magoo asked if I had a pillowcase for it.

"Nope," I answered, "I only have the one I'm already using."

It was almost Count, so things were quiet on the wing, and suddenly it seemed like every surrounding bunk was paying attention.

Magoo reached into his locker.

"Here. I got an extra t-shirt you can stuff it into."

Everyone understood that Magoo was trying to make up for the orange incident.

I took the obviously clean t-shirt and examined it skeptically.

"I don't know, Magoo... I usually don't sleep 'after' straight guys."

Everyone laughed, including him.

This is definitely becoming my specialty. The comeback that is neither too hot nor too cold, but just right.

I am halfway through my incarceration. If I can just stay in the Goldilocks Zone, I think I'll make it out of here okay.

A Kind of Heartburn

An hour ago, I got ready to take a shower and laid my toiletries out on my bed. Just then another neighbor from a bunk across from mine, Angel, asked if he could ask me something.

Angel looks like a younger, Latin version of Ben Kingsley, with a similarly deliberate and gentle manner. He has one of those smiles that warms up an offbeat face to make it positively handsome. I answered, "Sure," thinking that perhaps this would be the continuation of a conversation we had earlier about AIDS transmission.

Instead, Angel asked, "Do you ever wake up in the morning with this, you know, bad feeling in your stomach?"

I thought for a second.

"You mean that moment when your eyes open, and you re-alize again that it's not some dream, that you really did fuck up your life so bad that you actually landed in prison, and you still can't believe you're here, and you're afraid and guilt-ridden and nervous, and all you can think is that you'd give anything just to be able to close the door when you go to the bathroom and sleep in your own bed?"

A slow grin spread across his face.

"Yeah, like that."

I picked up my shaving kit and started off to the bathroom.

"Nope. Never."

Right and Wrong

I truly had to have been one of the shortest kids ever to play Little League. I remember Mr. Sewell, our coach, yelling, "Don't be afraid of the ball!" but of course, I was afraid of the ball, it was almost as big as my head. Even when I was lucky and the ball smacked dead into my glove, it stung my palm. Or it bounced off my middle finger or my head or a body part. Damn right I was afraid of the ball. The ball hurt.

Blessedly, Coach Sewell buried me in far right field most of the time, where I rarely had to make use my dismal fielding skills. I did better at bat because I was so short that if I crouched just a little, it was nearly impossible not to walk me. And I was a fast little bugger when it came to rounding the bases, so I did actually manage to do my part not to embarrass the Glenora Gators.

But we were a winning team largely because of the Sewell boys, Mel and Mike, the sons of the coach. I had a giant crush on Mel. He was a nine-year-old Robert Redford, replete with sandy windblown hair, Nordic blue eyes, and a gee-whiz smile. Mel was dreamy.

More than anything, I wanted to be Mel's best friend, and there were moments when I felt close to it, like that Saturday afternoon we played Time Tunnel together. The best part was rolling around like James Darren and Anthony Franciosa as they tumbled through that cheesy kaleidoscopic tunnel into yet a different century. I loved to tumble with Mel.

Unfortunately, Mel was a year older than me, and in the stratified rules of pre-adolescence, the difference of a year in age could make friendship between a second and a third-grader the equivalent of a mixed marriage. Mike, however, was my age, and we'd been in the same class since kindergarten. So I mostly played with him, while secretly pining for Mel, even though I was secretly relieved that our age difference made a friendship less viable. It was easier to worship him from afar than worry about whether he liked me as much as I liked him.

Mike was nice enough, but resented the effortless attention showered on Mel, and already had quite a chip on his shoulder. He also had the quick temper of his father, who'd done very well selling insurance, or so Mike emphatically believed.

"My Dad's a millionaire!" Mike exclaimed one day in the Sewell basement rec room, just after obliterating me in a game of pool. (We were ping-pong people across the street.)

"Are you sure?" I asked, reasonably certain that there were no millionaires in our neighborhood.

"Uh-huh!" Mike insisted defensively, as if I'd called him a dirty liar. "He's in the Millionaires Club! He told my mom and has a certificate and everything!"

A certificate! Well, that sealed it!

Coach Sewell scared me a little, but I liked his manliness and vaguely felt that if my Dad were more like him than I would be more like Mel; tousled and athletic without even trying. When I told my father that Mike's dad was a millionaire, it was almost a reproach. Take that, you pipe-smoking, chair-bound reader of the New York Times.

My Dad sighed his real-world sigh, probably debating whether to violate some code of suburbia by enlightening me about the true nature of his neighbor's finances.

"What he did, son, was sell a million dollars' worth of insurance. That doesn't make him a millionaire."

Of course, I couldn't understand the difference, so my Dad had to try to explain insurance to a eight-year-old, which almost made me cry. He finally gave up, leaving me relieved but also unable to challenge Mike's assertion. Later I did hear him say, while talking to my mother during their nightly ritual of sipping cocktails as she made dinner (him — two bourbons with a splash of

Wink; her; one Wink with a splash of bourbon), "The kid thinks his Dad is a millionaire, and meanwhile his name is on a list of Lakewood Country Club members who haven't paid their dues." (We weren't members, but somehow this neighborhood gossip had found its way to my father's ears.)

I made an attempt to refute to Mike his allegation about his father's income, but wilted in the face of his need to believe that his dad was a rich man. This probably correlated with the turmoil going on behind closed doors at the Sewells. You can bet there were a few strained conversations between the Coach and his pert wife Dottie before the shiny new Mustang in the Sewell driveway was repossessed not too much later. Of course, when my father explained the car's disappearance, I didn't understand what repossessed meant any more than how life insurance worked. Either way, I didn't care what Coach Sewell did or didn't own or earn. What I coveted was the masculinity that he and his sons possessed.

My Dad was a portly birdwatcher who'd been his high school's team equipment manager. "Bosco for Beebe" (his mother's maiden name was also his middle name) had been the chant from the stands during his adolescence. It impresses me now that my father shared such history nakedly. I wonder if he was preparing me for the self-doubt I would endure when I realized I was different from other boys.

We made it to the championships during the last year I played with the Glenora Gators, spearheaded by the hitting and fielding of the Sewell boys. In the final game, I got walked twice and bunted once for a base hit. I was watching from the bench by the time we reached the 9th inning.

We were behind at 11–10. Mel hit a long drive to the back of the field. He rounded first and second and continued past third, blazing. Only Mel himself realized his foot didn't touch third base.

He caught it and ran back a step to tag the base, then charged on just as the ball was thrown home. He slid in, tagged out at the very last second.

We were aghast, disbelieving. But... But... But...

Since we lived right across the street, I rode home with the Sewells, sitting in the back seat next to Mike, who glanced at me nervously as his father and brother debated.

"But, son, the ref didn't see you."

"But, Dad, I missed the plate."

"You could have made home."

"But, Dad, I missed the plate!"

Mel wanted badly for his father to tell him it didn't matter if we lost the game, that what mattered was that he did the right thing. But his father couldn't. The faux-millionaire with the re-possessed Mustang, the insurance salesman up from a depression childhood in Beckley, West Virginia, felt the sting of second place more than pride in his son for doing the right thing.

For him, winning was always the right thing.

The next morning on the back porch, I vainly trumpeted Coach Sewell's argument. I tried to tell my dad about how unfair it was that the Gators had lost, "even though Mel had rounded the plate." It was as good as tagged, wasn't it?

My dad refused to engage in such lofty philosophical digressions. He simply handed me his binoculars and said, "Look at that red-winged blackbird out there."

I attempted to argue; frustrated that he didn't agree with me that we should have won. But my father wouldn't take the bait, not even to weigh in on whether Mel had done the right thing by going back to tag third for sure.

I think my father wanted me to understand that in the grand scheme of things, it made precious little difference whether one group of boys rounded some bases more times than another group of boys. However, teaching one boy to appreciate nature — that was important.

So I took the binoculars and looked through them, and

stopped thinking about the game. And in that moment, it felt completely right that he was my father, and I didn't envy Mel, his golden boy looks or his millionaire Dad.

PART THREE
Redwood

Bali Hai

Well, I finally got transferred to Redwood Hall. Barring something unforeseen, this is where I will be spending the next 86 days, two hours, 34 minutes and 11 seconds until my release. Not that I'm counting down or anything.

The physical structure is the same as at Cedar — four wings extending from a central Day Room, guard office, lavatory and showers. There are 50 men to a wing, in bunk beds lining each hall, with standing lockers next to each bunk.

This new dorm feels even less tense than Cedar. Mostly, I think, because there's a lot less boredom. A fair amount of guys have jobs, and there's a lot of reading because we have regular access to a library. The prison economy is far more robust, as well, as tobacco is available along with items received in quarterly care packages, as well as from monthly canteen.

My first night here I fell asleep blessedly early, but the drop in temperature woke me up in the middle of the night. Luckily, I had an extra blanket I was using as a pillow. I also closed the window closest to the bunk, but as I tried to get back to sleep, I couldn't shake the unpleasant scent of manure wafting in.

On the way to breakfast, I noticed that some of the grounds were being reseeded, so thought it might just be the smell of fertilizer. "Hell, no," an older, thoroughly grizzled inmate told me. "Chino used to be cow pasture. That's gonna wake you up every single day."

It's positively comical how they called our two weeks in Cedar "orientation" when they didn't even hand out so much as a flyer detailing new routines and procedures, or how they were going to change. There, a med-tech came to the dorm to dispense meds during Pill Call. Now we have 30 minutes, twice a day, to cross the grounds to the infirmary. When I discovered this, the annoyed guard, a certain Miss Baylor, wrote me out a late pass, adding tartly, "We don't hold your hand over here."

I held my tongue and just said "thank you".

I did enjoy my very first walk unescorted across the prison compound, past the baseball diamond and basketball courts (just like the brochure promised!). The med-tech gave me a requisite frown for being late, but didn't have much choice but to dispense my pills.

I finally had a chance to have a real conversation with my new bunkie, who's been working and sleeping most of the past two days. Steve is around my age, bald, and reminds me a little bit of one of those B-movie actors from the '40s who always played the best friend or sidekick. He's sort of gruff and good-natured at the same time, as well as disarmingly honest about being here for trafficking in stolen merchandise in order to finance his crystal meth habit. I told him I completely understood that particular addiction, while adding (quite truthfully) that I blessedly neither miss the drug nor have any desire to go back to it.

"Not me," Steve said bouncily. "The first thing I'm going to do when I get out is shoot up." (As if I needed a visual aid, he mimed that last part as well.)

He might as well have been Ray Walston in *South Pacific*, describing the buxom gal waiting for him at the pier the very first day of shore leave.

At least I have started to make a new friend, and he's one of "my people" at that. Earl is obviously gay, but was a married, suburban dad for many years. This history is less the reason he has managed to "pass" as straight here than because he puts the word "fucking" before everything, including the gayest of statements, i.e., "You're not in fucking Kansas anymore, Dorothy."

Earl is in his '30s, with lovely green eyes, and would be handsome if not for an incredibly weak chin. He also has a brazen self-confidence that borders on cluelessness. He's the type who'll find out that someone he's been trying to call collect has put a block on his phone, and insists there has to be some mistake, so writes them instead. (I would crawl into a hole and cry for three days if I thought someone specifically made sure that he wouldn't have to take my calls.)

Earl will ask you to be discreet about his being HIV+, and then tell a relative stranger about it 20 minutes later. His hyperactive and contradictory nature gives me pause about becoming close to him; at the same time, he's probably the only openly gay friend I'm going to find in here. And he can be rather funny, which usually trumps everything else for me anyway.

He's here for selling meth, of course. (I wonder what gay men used to go to prison for?)

Où est la Bibliotèque?

I finally got to the library today. It isn't half bad. I took out Isak Dinesen's *Out of Africa* and, bizarrely enough, the teacher's manual for *Son et Sens,* a high school textbook we used in 10th grade French. I can hear my mother's voice as I read it, and this comforts me. I also withdrew a few bestsellers by old dependables like John Grisham and Susan Isaacs. Nothing beats good, escapist storytelling when you're locked up. I can't remember who said, "Good writers are good readers," but he or she was definitely on to something.

The clerk checking out my books was a handsome fellow named Armando, and I inquired about how hard/easy it was to get a job in the library. I already knew the answer — I have way too little time left to get such a plum assignment — but he seemed to enjoy having the conversation. In fact, I think he may have been flirting with me.

I realize that I need to evaluate how I used substances to do "the work" involved in meeting guys. I always let the buzz relax me, loosen my tongue, lower my inhibitions (and my zipper.) Any other approach seemed like such an inefficient use of available resources. In other words, I was incredibly lazy.

Even the brief exchange with Armando got me completely flustered in a way I frankly haven't *felt* for years — at least not without numbing or enhancing that sensation almost immediately. I literally have not allowed myself to just "be" with feelings of anxiety, depression, excitement or joy for the better part of two decades. (In my defense, the AIDS years were awful — loss after loss after loss. There was a lot you didn't want to feel.)

Well, I guess if I can learn how not to medicate my feelings in here, I can do it anywhere.

But to be on the safe side, I may have to stay away from men for, I don't know, a decade or two.

Up, Up, and Away

Six dorms use the same mess hall, 15 minutes to eat each, staggered over the two hours allotted for breakfast and dinner. So if there is any trouble anywhere, say a fight, it can result in traffic jams everywhere getting to breakfast. Today we left a half-hour late and then were held up again en route, which meant standing around in a field, shooting the shit, stomachs growling.

This morning we'd been standing behind the baseball diamond for a good five minutes, though a lucky few at least had the fence behind home plate to lean on. Some of us noticed a red-tailed hawk circling above. It was so majestic that one by one we started nudging each other, wondering out loud if the hawk was as hungry as we were.

Almost as if she was waiting for the attention of every inmate before she dived, the hawk suddenly made a sharp, swooping descent toward the field to our left. A vole no one had seen was scampering from one hole to another as fast as its scared little feet could take it. Poor thing didn't have a chance. The hawk expertly slowed her acceleration just in time for her claws to pluck the rodent off the ground, and with nary so much as a bye-your-leave, continued into the trees with the futilely squirming rodent in her clutches, probably to be fed her chicks.

One of us (well, me) broke out in applause, joined instantly by everyone else in line in both directions.

It was all anyone talked about over breakfast.

All Over the Place

In prison, R&R does not stand for Rest & Relaxation, but Receiving & Release. It's where you go the morning you are freed ("Release"). Until then, it's where you go to pick up packages ("Receiving"). First you receive a notice that the package has arrived. Then you wait for another slip (a "ducat") telling you to come pick it up.

Unfortunately, an inmate delivers these notifications, so the entire dorm learned at the same time I did that my first quarterly package had arrived. Steve (my bunkie) suggested that I order a lock since they do not come with our lockers. It might seem strange, but theft is actually rare here because everyone knows if you are caught you will be thrashed within an inch of your life, maybe worse. So I asked Steve why he thought I needed a lock. It turns out that there is a double standard when it comes to gay inmates, who are often "taxed" just for being gay. To boot, he'd heard some scuttlebutt that this might be the case with me.

Along with sexual assault, of course, this is the kind of bullshit every gay man fears will happen to him in prison. It threw me into a bit of a tizzy, but I also sensed that if they were going to do it, they wouldn't have bothered letting me hear about it through Steve in advance. They wanted to see if they could scare me into offering them the package, which was a lot less messy than having to take it from me. It's your basic protection racket.

Steve confirmed that this was how it worked, and I suddenly wondered if he was in on it in some way. Not because he has anything against me personally, or gays, for that matter, but because I think he is doing meth in here and could easily owe money for it. (I suspect this because he is often awake, reading, when I go to the bathroom in the middle of the night.)

Still, it sucked not to be sure whether I could really trust him. We haven't exactly become friends, but he's been friendly enough. He even got excited when he found out my last name, because his (gay) brother is a landscape designer, and Steve said he would get a kick out of knowing I was related to Frederick Law Olmsted.

I decided to ask Earl for advice. That meant pushing past his initial response, which is always "don't worry about it" no matter what the issue. He could tell that pissed me off in this case, so he made a little bit of effort after that, as he can't stand for anybody to be mad at him.

"Well, let them know you'll put up a fight, then."

"But I won't. You know I'm pathologically non-violent."

"Yeah, but does Steve know that? He's the one who'll be sending a message back to these pricks. If he thinks you mean it, they'll believe you mean it."

Oddly enough, one of the few conversations Steve and I had of much length was on this topic exactly, when we talked about childrearing. He thought spanking was perfectly normal and I thought it was harmful and unnecessary. (This could be one of the reasons he doesn't seem to get much mail from any of his ten kids. That's right — ten kids. And three ex-wives.)

But there was something about me that Steve probably suspected but I haven't actually confirmed — the reason I go to Pill Call every day.

"Well," I told Steve, "obviously if there are three of them and one of me, I'm going to lose. But they're taking a pretty big risk."

"How so?"

I leaned over so no one could hear us.

" 'Cause I'll put up just enough of a fight to make sure I bleed. *Profusely.*"

I generally avoid looking directly into someone's eyes in this place, but I held Steve's gaze long enough for him to see that I was deadly serious (emphasis on *deadly).*

They were trying to scare me into handing over my shit, so I took my fear and found a way to hand it right back to them. My most satisfying moment in prison by far. Indeed, this morning Steve told me that I didn't have anything to worry about, which made the trip to R&R a lot like real R&R.

I now have the watch, the sneakers, and the Walkman-radio. We are just close enough to Pasadena for me to pick up KPCC rather well. Finally, I can follow the election, and every other bit of news I've been missing about a world that keeps spinning despite my silent entreaties that it would freeze during my, er, sabbatical.

I have also given away four shots of coffee, two to the guys who I think were the ones conspiring to tax me.

Sometimes revenge is a dish best served hot.

The Defense Rests

"Tank" is a stocky, mustachioed guy who has taken it upon himself to watch over the dorm from his top bunk perch at the front of D-wing. He's like that kid in junior high who insists that one of his duties as student council vice-president is to monitor the cafeteria at lunch, a task he actually makes up to cover for the fact that no one wants to eat with him.

Every night, Tank lays claim to "first watch," making sure we all know that only his vigilance keeps the plotting black hordes from putting into motion their evil plans to shank all the white inmates in our sleep. Even the hard-core skinheads roll their eyes at Tank — which is not to say that they don't find him useful here and there (guarding a pruno stash, for example). But no one hangs out with him, that's for sure.

This morning, Tank signaled me into his "driveway" (the area to the left of one's bunk) and motioned me to sit on his bed. (Later, I described it to Earl as "the Director of Human Resources asking me to step into his office for a little chat." Earl howled.) It annoyed me, but as I am still negotiating my place in the pecking order here, I thought it best to see what he had to say.

Basically, he wanted credit for calling off the tax-the-fag party, even though it may well have been his suggestion in the first place. When I demurred on showing gratitude for the right to receive packages unmolested, he switched gears, explaining that the real problem hadn't been that I was gay, but that I'd come to Redwood from Birch — the protective custody dorm. In this scenario, the suspicion was that I could be a plant, and he just "wanted to make sure" that wasn't the case.

I was pretty certain this was bullshit. If I'd been in Birch as a result of being an informant elsewhere, they wouldn't have sent me back out into gen-pop to do more informing. That would be like an undercover cop going back into the Mafia after his cover was blown. It didn't make sense.

He didn't deserve any reassurance, but I gave it to him anyway just to be on the safe side. "No, Tank. I did not go to Birch because I was an informer, and am certainly not one now. But let me just point out that if I were, I would hardly tell you I was, right?"

"Er... right. I guess."

"And if I *wasn't gay* or HIV+, I sure wouldn't lie and say I was, would I?"

He thought about that for a second.

Keep up with me, Tank.

"No... I guess not."

I had the odd sensation, suddenly, of winding up a summation in front of a jury.

"So you can probably pretty safely conclude that I was in Birch because where I was before then, Sycamore, was dangerous for someone like me."

"You were in Sycamore?"

"I would have told you if you'd asked. I don't lie."

This had not always been true, exactly, but it was true now.

"Well, I don't lie either," Tank added defensively.

"Good. Then, you can tell me, truthfully, if I'm going to have any more trouble in this dorm. 'Cause if I have to worry about getting jumped or any shit like that, I will roll myself up and go back to Birch tonight."

Poor Tank. He was completely unprepared to be on the receiving end of the interrogation.

"No... you're cool."

"That's good to know, I appreciate it."

I stood up, as if I was the one who had initiated the conversation and was now satisfied with how it had ended.

"Nice talking with you, Tank."

He nodded, frankly unsure of what had happened. I daresay his plan had been for me to leave thinking I owed him a debt of some kind, and if anything, he felt exactly the opposite.

Head First

Last night I was offered my first line of speed since my incarceration. I declined. I also turned down a swig of Pruno, and two offers of pot. I just kept my focus on what I wanted to do last night and today, and that included writing two letters, indulging in my new colored pencil set, and fashioning "shelves" (of cardboard) in my locker to accommodate the stuff that just arrived in my quarterly package. I truly "get" that none of these activities would be more enjoyable or better accomplished under the influence of some kind of substance.

It helped that Wizard, a young Latino who has taken a shine to me, had just reinforced what a stupid move it is to do drugs here. He is getting out in two weeks, and he claims that if he doesn't come up with the $400 he owes to his supplier, he might be leaving "feet first."

He told me this as a prelude to asking me if he could borrow $50. Evidently, Wizard seems to think I haven't been paying attention to the workings of the prison economy. No one fronts anybody $400 worth of drugs unless they are 100% sure they will get it back. Of course, they would prefer it sooner rather than later, but they will have no trouble sending someone to a parolee's house after he gets out, and you can be sure the debt will be doubled if that happens. I feel sorry for Wizard's family in this situation, but damned if I was going to find some goons looming over me the day after his release, insisting that Wizard assured them I'd be good for the balance. Not to mention, the Woods would make my life a living hell for loaning money across racial/ ethnic lines if I did. That's precisely the kind of stupid shit that starts riots.

I was annoyed at Wizard's attempt to blatantly manipulate me, but I couldn't manage to stay mad. That's because I strongly suspect that he is struggling with his sexuality, and I feel bad for him. His world, sadly, will accept his law-breaking, even his drug addiction, with far more equanimity than any hint of homosexuality. It's not much of an exaggeration to say that when he gets out, he will just be in a different kind of prison, otherwise known as the closet.

One of the reasons I've been increasingly "out" here — more than I would have ever thought I would be — is that I truly am the only person some of these guys have ever met who operates unapologetically in life as an openly gay person. This is especially true of the black and Latino inmates, who were overwhelmingly raised in evangelical or devout Catholic households. Most of them have completely swallowed the propaganda that being gay is an exclusively white disease to which they are constitutionally immune as men of color. It's not that they haven't met men who have sex with men, or even done so themselves in some cases, but the notion that it needn't be a secret kept at all costs is virtually unimagined. It's not my sexuality that amazes them, but they are genuinely perplexed as to why I don't feel bad about.

This curiosity may be why they seem relatively comfortable asking me questions that are far more personal than those they would ask any other white guy here. And as long as they don't start grandstanding to let everyone know that they think I'm a sinner, I am generally patient with them. (After all, black and brown people have been putting up with all sorts of ignorant inquiries from white people for centuries.)

I don't even try to restrict the conversation to the earshot of the person asking the questions — rather the opposite. That's because the specific information I am sharing is far less important than how I share it. I want everyone to hear the lack of shame in my voice when I say "of course," my family knows I am gay; I want them to see my matter-of-fact demeanor when I answer honestly, "No, I wouldn't take a pill to change if I could."

This last observation was greeted skeptically by D-Roll, who occupies the bunk next to mine. We became friendly when he offered to buy any extra batteries I had at a fairly good price in packets of ramen, an exchange of goods and services that is small-scale enough not to ruffle any feathers with the Woods hierarchy. His pitch was direct and energetic, very early Richard Pryor, "Hey, listen, I'm a hustler, that's what I do. It's in my blood, and it's what I'll always do, in jail and out. But I'm a fair hustler and I'll be fair with you!"

When he completed our transaction, he anointed me "square." Later, he asked me if I'd really meant it.

"Meant what?"

"You seriously wouldn't take a pill to be straight?"

"I seriously wouldn't."

He puts both hands up. "I'm just asking..."

I mirrored the same gesture back to him, "I'm just answering!"

We Reserve the Right

I got a job assignment as a porter. That means cleaning the bath-room twice a day and sweeping and mopping the hallways once a day, five days a week. This last part makes me a little nervous, be-cause it will send me into the other three wings, full of unfamiliar personalities. For example, there are guys who are completely anal about their "driveway", and will get bent out of shape if you clean it. Also, you have to be careful not to appear to see or hear things you might actually be seeing or hearing.

Cleaning the bathroom is just unpleasant, but you do get to hose it down, which Earl tells me is actually fun. He's been doing this for two weeks already, and we'll even be doing some shifts together.

We do a lot together — going to Pill Call, the library, and Yard, for example. And every day we eat lunch together, which consists of the meager P&J they hand out at breakfast along with something from my canteen stash, usually soup. I supply it and Earl prepares it, and we use my top bunk as our table. Of course, we unfailingly offer a bite to some of our brethren, knowing full well they can't take us up on it.

"Are you sure?" I ask innocently. "No? Okay, but it really is good. Earl makes the best *cross-dressing.*"

They pause, unsure if they heard right, then mutter some-thing and shamble on. (This is actually very mean of us, because some of them really are hungry. That's actually a big reason in-mates take serious risks smuggling and dealing drugs here. If you don't have anyone on the outside to put money on your books, you will simply not get enough to eat in prison.)

Oddly enough, Earl and I do not eat breakfast or dinner to-gether. That's because Earl already had a dinner "buddy" before

177

I got to the dorm, a straight guy named Don who is cool eating with one gay guy, but not two. According to the stupid math of this place, eating with two of us would be definitive proof that he's one of us.

Therefore, I eat alone. That sounds sad and lonely, but I swear it's not. Not only do I not have to tolerate what would be largely brain-dead conversation, but I get to read *The New Yorker* undisturbed. In fact, I get a big kick out of knowing that I am almost certainly the only person in the history of the California prison system to have ever read *The Talk of the Town* while chowing down on "Unpardoned Turkey Tacos."

I admit this one-gay-at-a-time rule of Don's pisses me off. More specifically, why doesn't Earl tell Don to just screw himself? Earl argues that he'll be here four months longer than I will and needs every friend he can get. He has a point, but I still needle him mercilessly over it.

The other day he got very defensive. "I don't have a sister who's blogging what I write, either!" Which was funny in and of itself because, despite my explanations, he really has no idea what a blog is.

If the culture weren't so racist here, I would no doubt be eating with some of the Latinos or blacks, but that just isn't done. I'm sure the barrier will fall one day, but I very much doubt a gay inmate will be the one to break it.

Neighbors

Although the races do not eat together and only bunk with each other, we are not clustered geographically in a dorm, i.e., blacks on one end, whites on the other, and Latins yet somewhere else. In fact, there are rarely two bunks of the same race next to each other. The distribution is more likely — black / white / black / Latin / white / black / Latin / black / Latin, etc. Because of this configuration, there is more *de facto* socializing between races than one might think, simply by virtue of the sleeping arrangements. That is how I've begun to get to know the two African-American pairs of bunkmates to my right and to my left.

On one side are Sharif (bottom bunk) and Phil (top bunk). Sharif is an autodidact who fancies himself the spiritual love child of Malcolm X and Bob Marley, although his attachment to conspiracy theories concerning AIDS and 9/11 certainly don't suggest much intellectual rigor. That said, he definitely does *think* about things, which is more than can be said for a lot of the men here.

Phil, on the other hand, couldn't be more down-to-earth. He's naturally observant and funny, and doesn't take himself near as seriously as Sharif. But he's also prone to depression. One day I saw him lying on his bunk, just staring at the ceiling, so I asked if he wanted to borrow a book to read. He declined, saying that reading gave him a headache. I asked if maybe he needed glasses, and gradually he revealed that his sight was fine, but that the words "jumbled up" on him.

Twenty minutes later I had managed to convince Phil that he might be suffering from undiagnosed dyslexia. Not surprisingly, in all these years he'd never even heard the word. He had heard "learning disability," but I also sensed that was a loaded term that he'd probably been bludgeoned into Special Ed with. So I emphasized that anyone could be dyslexic and that anyone could overcome it. He seemed skeptical. So I told him a teensy weensy little lie — that I'd struggled with it myself.

Okay, it was a big lie, but God forgives me, I know she does. No one I knew who has overcome dyslexia would have meant anything to him — but he sees me every day, doing practically nothing but read and write.

Besides, this was probably the only chance we'd even have to talk about it. Sharif is almost always around, and Phil would never want him to know he has difficulty reading. In fact, Phil told me that was the reason he never said no to a game of Monopoly, which he and Sharif play for hours upon hours.

"I'm afraid he's going to show me that book he's writing, man! Shit, I even let him cheat, just to keep the game going."

He's very resourceful, Phil.

I've mentioned my neighbor on the other side, D-Roll. Yesterday, I was returning from morning Pill Call, and D-Roll comes up next to me, doing his people-to-see, places-to-go strut. He says, "C'mon, Square, put some get in your go, and walk with me!" This is fairly rare occurrence between races, but if you have the same destination, you can get away with it.

I asked him how it is that he seems to have so much leeway to travel between dorms to carry out his various hustles. In response, he pulled out a piece of paper that has been folded and unfolded many times. It was a pass that details his status as an umpire for the prison softball league. Of course, there's hardly a softball game underway near as often as D-roll is out and about, but he's the type to lie with such conviction they no doubt let him pass like the stormtroopers in Star Wars when Obi-wan Kenobi says, "These aren't the droids you're looking for."

I asked him why his nickname is "D-Roll" and he told me the following story. "When I was 8, I used to have a thing with this 15-year-old ho', and we used to do the 'nasty.' No kidding, a couple of times a week, and she would give me a dollar every time." (D-Roll is about my age, so this would have been 1966.) "And back then I used to sell candy bars — I was a hustler from the very beginning, so I did well — and between what I made and what she gave me, I always had a roll of dollar bills. So when this bitch would see me, she'd say, 'Hey, D, where's your roll?' And that's how I got the name D-Roll!"

D-Roll's old bunkie was determined to sleep away his sentence on Seroquel and snored a lot, so I was happy to see him leave. But his new bunkie is simply one of the oddest birds, bar none, that I have ever met in prison or elsewhere, for that matter.

He will definitely earn an entry of his own, but I am still gathering data, like an ornithologist who doesn't want to claim he's found a new species until he's absolutely sure.

Political Prisoner

I received a ducat informing me there was a package from my friend Claudia waiting for me at R&R. This was a little strange, because all books must be sent directly from the publisher, and the original sender is usually not indicated on the notice to pick it up.

The officer who runs R&R is named Sargent Erlichson, and he is right out of Central Casting, replete with a ruddy complexion and potbelly. Think Rod Steiger in *The Heat of the Night,* minus the southern drawl.

The Sargent looked at the slip and made a small, disapproving sound, like the sigh a parent lets out when a report card confirms an expected B-minus. Ominously, he motioned me to follow him into the bowels of the mailroom. There he handed me a booklet detailing the regulations governing the receipt and distribution of packages in the California Department of Corrections.

"Ever read that?"

As a matter of fact, I had, only because my sister had printed much of it off the Internet and mailed it to me. But I wasn't going to tell him that.

"Sargent, I've gone through three separate 'orientations,' and these rules weren't on any bulletin board, or passed out to us, or anything, so, no, I haven't read it."

"So read them now."

There were three stapled pages, back and front.

"Now? You want me to read them now?"

"I'll wait. I've got plenty to do."

He started opening parcels with a box cutter and looking through them. On a shelf behind him I could see Claudia's handwriting on the oversized envelope she'd sent me containing whatever mysterious contents Erlichson thought suspicious enough to be busting my balls over.

I protested. "There's no way she would have sent me any contraband. Can you just tell me what the problem is?"

He pointed to Regulation 110c (or whatever). "Right there. 'Magazines are to be sent directly from the publisher.'"

Was that all? I explained helpfully that I was only going to be here until November, so it made sense that my friend didn't want to buy an entire subscription just to share a few articles.

The Sargent took the parcel addressed to me off the shelf, and slowly spilled its contents onto the table. They consisted of an issue of *Mother Jones and Atlantic Monthly* each, accompanied by a neatly typed letter from Claudia.

I suppressed the urge to ask if he thought *Mother Jones* was some kind of maternal fetish porn. It struck me as very unlikely that he had even come across either magazine before, but it turned out their editorial direction wasn't the problem anyway.

The problem was Claudia's cover note, which was lying slightly askew on top of *The Atlantic.*

"I don't read the letters, but I have to scan them, in case there are terrorist threats... Like your friend here says she doesn't like George Bush..."

What the fuck? Did he really just say that?

After I picked my jaw up off the floor, I saw the sentence that had jumped out at the Sargent because of one word in caps, *"I did NOT listen to Bush's speech..."*

I pointed out that the GOP convention had just been held. "Are you saying she might be an extremist because she didn't listen to the President's speech?"

I wish I could do justice to the Sargent's rambling, incoherent answer — it was worthy of a minor Dickens character, Barnabas Bucklesby, or somesuch. Suffice to say, as Erlichson was making the nonsensical point that "we have to know you approve of the material they're sending you," I noticed the distinct whiff of alcohol on his breath.

Well, well, well.

As the Sargent yammered on, I remembered the time I was stuck on a flight to Luxembourg next to a recently discharged Marine who claimed he had a fear of flying that only four screwdrivers could calm. He went on, and on, each cocktail making him more garrulous and driving me closer to contemplating murder at 30,000 feet. I was sure I'd lost him at the baggage claim, only to run into him on the train to Paris, where he switched places just to sit next to his "buddy from the plane."

Funny how some memories migrate from one filing cabinet to another over the years; that annoying young man I couldn't wait to escape two decades ago was suddenly someone I'd gladly buy a couple of drinks.

Sargent Erlichson repeated himself, a tad irritated.

"I asked you a question, Olmsted."

"I'm sorry. What?"

"Are you a Republican or a Democrat?"

"Are you serious?"

"Well, you know…I have to do my job."

"What does my party affiliation have to do with your job?"

"It doesn't matter, or anything, I'm just curious."

"Respectfully," I said, my voice dripping with disrespect, "it's none of your damn business."

"Well, these magazines were not sent the right way, so…"

"Are you saying to get my magazines I have to tell you how I vote?"

"Only if you want to. I'm just trying to have a conversation."

I'm just trying to have a conversation. I can take a lot, but an inane platitude will push me over the edge, every time.

"A pretty unconstitutional conversation! Or it would be, if I had any rights, but oops, I forgot! I'm in prison! I have no rights!"

Oh, well, I thought, I can kiss those magazines goodbye now. But the Sargent seemed unperturbed by my sarcasm. He was finally having his "conversation," I guess.

"Let me explain something... You're in prison; there are a lot of assholes in prison. Some guys will stab you for a pack of cigarettes. I'm asking you that question to find out if you have any character."

I seemed to be stranded in the Land of Non-Sequitur. I had to figure out the magic words to get out of there.

"So wait... you wanted to see if I would refuse to answer the question? That would mean I had character?'"

He squinted in confusion.

"No, the other way around!"

I guess sometimes a stupid question is just a stupid question.

"I'm a Democrat."

"There you go!"

He basked triumphantly in his breakthrough, until I reminded him why I was there.

"Can I have my magazines now?"

"Oh... right."

He slid them back in the envelope, and handed it to me, clearly disappointed that our "conversation" had come to an end.

I barely made it back to the dorm in time for Pill Call. I was all set to tell Earl this crazy-ass story, but way across the yard, I saw none other than Starr, moving across the field like a giraffe crossing the savannah.

I realized that Earl wouldn't really appreciate my tale of mailroom censorship anyway, so I told him all about her instead.

Persona Grata

I forget to mention that this weekend, I was joined at dinner by Jersey, one of the porters I work with. At first, I was afraid I was getting punk'd, but then his bunkie, Viper, also sat down, friendly as can be. Since then, I haven't eaten alone once. Just like that, I am finally the gay who came in from the cold.

Yesterday morning, a new guy joined us. He was greeted as something of a conquering hero; the prodigal son returned. I pieced together that he'd been released on parole just a few weeks before I arrived, and was now back on a violation. This is how Viper introduced us:

"Jimmy, this is Mark. He's gay, but he's all right!" Realizing how that sounded, he added a slightly sturdier endorsement. "Mark offers you coffee before you even have to ask." (This is true. I can always tell when someone's hoping for a shot.)

"And he cleans toilets better than I ever will!" added Jersey, meaning it as a compliment. Jimmy seemed to look at me for elaboration.

"My mom made all of us learn how," I explained. "In fact, one of my best customers said to me once, 'Mark, the reason I like to buy drugs from you is that your bathroom is always spotless.'"

Viper thought that was hysterical.

"Man, you kill me."

I was trying to play it cool, as if I barely noticed Jimmy's movie star looks. He's got dark wavy hair, deep-set blue eyes, and a completely rakish grin. Soap opera handsome.

He's also very competitive.

"You want funny? I'll give you funny."

He proceeded to tell this joke:

A man came home for lunch from work, and discovered his pet

186

Rottweiler had somehow gotten hold of the neighbor's rabbit, and 'playing' with it, had killed it. The man was mortified but was at least able to get the rabbit from his dog before too much obvious damage was done.

Sneaking over to his neighbors, he put the rabbit against its water bowl and hoped against hope they would believe the rabbit had expired naturally.

When he came home from work later that day, the police were in front of his neighbor's house.

"What happened?" he asked fearfully.

The cop answered, "The kid's rabbit died and they buried it in the backyard. Some SICKO dug it up and propped it against the water bowl for the kids to find when they got home from school!"

I wish I could include Jimmy's malleable facial expressions — he really knew how to make that old chestnut extremely funny. I was so caught up, I only noticed just as we were collecting our trays that someone else was now sitting alone in the mess hall, a new face I didn't recognize.

Enter Lynn

As soon as we got back to the dorm, I had to sweep and mop, and I found the recent arrival sitting on a bottom bunk in A-wing, petting Lil' Bit, the cat I thought belonged to Cedar Hall but evidently gets around. I reached out my hand.

"Hi. I'm Mark."

The transgender inmate I'd seen in the mess hall extended her hand warily, as if I might shock her with a buzzer.

"Lynn." Her voice was all gravel.

"Nice to meet you, Lynn."

"You know, you're the first fucking person here to say two words to me."

"How about your bunkie?"

"He asked to be moved. Ha!" she snorted derisively. "I'm glad."

This was the first time I'd heard of an inmate refusing to bunk with someone and getting away with it. Wow. That was just plain mean.

"Listen, I have to finish mopping up, but why don't you come over to my bunk in D-Wing before chow tonight. We can walk over together, and I can introduce you to Earl, too."

"Is he the babe you were eating breakfast with?"

"I wish. No, that's Jimmy, he just got here. Earl's not nearly as cute, but he's one of us."

I really did have to finish, so excused myself.

"I'll see you later, Lynn."

"Sure."

A few minutes later, just as I was finishing up, she tapped me on the shoulder.

"Hey, can I ask you a question?

"Sure."

"When do you think the best time is for me to take a shower?"

She didn't have to add, "alone."

I squeezed the mop into the bucket.

"Well, Lynn, you've come to the right place."

So that afternoon, when I cleaned the bathroom with Jersey, I told him I needed a huge favor that could get both of us in trouble, but was also kind of cool. This was exactly the right thing to tell Jersey, who wants nothing more than to be cool.

That's how we ended up sneaking Lynn into the showers as we cleaned the bathroom. It was a bit nerve-wracking, but she was extremely fast, and we pulled it off.

"You owe me one, dawg," Jersey told me afterwards.

That was the first time in prison I enjoyed being called "dawg."

At chow Earl stuck with Don, Jersey and Viper ate with Jimmy, and I was alone with Lynn. I made a little joke that we could start a band named *Pariahs Carey,* but Lynn didn't know what a pariah was, and I suddenly thought better of explaining it to her.

So here's the thing I haven't mentioned yet. Lynn is very homely. Her hair is gray and frizzy, and her teeth are yellow and intermittent. If it weren't for her small breast implants, you would just think she was an ugly 51-year-old man. Frankly, she reminds me of Montgomery Burns on *The Simpsons.* (I know, ouch.)

How she made a living as a prostitute in Ontario, California, is beyond me. I can only surmise that when she gets all dolled up, it is precisely her grotesquerie that turns them on. The dominatrix chick-with-a-dick is as far away as a suburban Dad can possibly get from his wholesome wife, I guess. Whatever fantasy Lynn appeals to, she made enough money to keep herself in crystal meth, and repeated arrests for solicitation and possession were finally enough to land her in here.

Here's the other thing. She may sound like a fascinating, Fellini-like character, but she is deadly boring. I've only eaten with her twice, and I have already run out of conversation. But as they say in the *the-a-hood,* sometimes you just have to commit. Once I decided to treat her like a human being, there was no turning back.

I'm not doing it for the scintillating conversation, anyway. I'm doing it because it's less uncomfortable than not doing it. Just walking to and from the mess hall means hearing all manner of lewd and nasty commentary from inmates going in the opposite direction — my bleeding heart could never take watching her endure that alone. Lynn half-heartedly throws back a one-liner here and there, but Oscar Wilde she is not. To the extent that I can provide a shield, if only by just walking next to her, I am glad. (The only remarks directed at me imply that I'm trying to get laid. It's too funny to be insulting.)

There seems to be a lesson or two the Goddesses insist I learn while I'm here. Something along the lines of it not always being about me.

(Ha! As if.)

P.S. I did ask if "on the streets" she always operates as a woman (yes) and if so, how regularly it is noted that she is "in transition." She answered, "Yeah, little kids... the brats... they always grab their mother and point and say, 'Mommy, that's a man!'"

The Ketchup Kid

So I promised to report back on my other neighbor, D-Roll's bunkie.

Adam is 6' 4" but thin as a beanpole, so not very intimidating. He never seems to comb his wiry, overgrown Afro, which I suppose is fashionable with other entitled 22-year-olds but just comes off as unkempt here. I have never seen an inmate so seemingly hell-bent on alienating everybody in the dorm, and less concerned about how truly dangerous this could be for him.

Adam is very light-skinned, but he is classified as black, and rule #1 of this place is to make friends with at least a few members of your own race. If that's too much to ask, you should at least avoid giving the unmistakable impression that you look down on them for being in prison in the first place. (Sounding extremely white is not particularly helpful either, especially with a penetrating nasal voice that carries your every snide remark halfway across the wing.)

I certainly get the whole fish-out-of-water thing, but I have also never pretended that I wasn't guilty as charged and didn't deserve to be here as much as anyone else. In fact, someone with all of my advantages in life has far fewer excuses than others do. And from what I can tell, the same should apply to Adam.

His father is a wealthy attorney in Boston and a major behind-the-scenes player in Republican politics there — so a big fish in a small pond, I guess. In fact, that's what first got us talking (well, arguing). He is the only person here as obsessed with the Presidential campaign as I am.

Adam is a passionate supporter of Bush, but could care less about his policies. He just wants to back the candidate he thinks will win. And Kerry, to his mind, is "a loser." When he says this, his implication is clear; anyone who supports him is a loser, too.

Although Reagan's a big favorite, Adam's true obsession is anything and everything related to the Kennedys. When I pointed out what seemed to me the obvious contradiction of waxing rhapsodic over the biggest liberal Democratic family in American history while holding the current party nominee in contempt, Adam sneered. Even D-Roll, who I don't think has ever seen the inside of a voting booth, chimed in that I had a point. But there is no talking rationally to Adam about any of this, and I have stopped trying.

Although some of this is guesswork, I think Adam was adopted into a wealthy white family, but his mother drank or did drugs when she was pregnant with him. I think he has been in trouble since he was a little boy, most often because of his penchant for pyromania. At the same time, he developed this notion that his father was grooming him for a political career, an option he still seems to think is possible even with a prison sentence for "aggravated mayhem" on his resume. He's repeatedly mentioned a cousin running for state assembly whose campaign he's going to work on when he gets out. That's when I realized that it isn't the politics of the Kennedys or Bushes that interest him, but the fact that they are political dynasties. His fantasy is to have a place at the table, to be the next in line, the heir apparent. And yet he seems devoid of any trait essential to a successful politician — a love of people, an ability to listen, an ounce of charm.

Those of us bunking near Adam realized he was bizarre right off the bat, but it wasn't obvious to everyone in the dorm until we had hamburgers and hotdogs for dinner — which Adam knew ahead of time because menus are posted weekly on the bulletin board.

Before chow, Adam went up and down all four of Redwood's wings, asking everybody to please give him any packets of ketchup they didn't use. (That sounds awfully polite. It was more like, "Give me your ketchup, okay!")

At first, I imagined this was the key ingredient to some bizarre Bloody Mary pruno he was making, but no, Adam claims he doesn't drink or do drugs. He just hoards this particular condiment.

After the ketchup culling, he held up a plastic bag full of packets and asserted, "I am a very shrewd businessman."

You should have seen the look on D-Roll's face. I may have to rename him "Eye-Roll."

Personal Business

Since I've been at Redwood, guards have asked me twice why I haven't been taking my pills, and twice I assured them I get my meds every day. Finally a third notice arrived, and they gave me a pass to go to the doctor's office to figure out what's happening.

It turns out that the notice was from the head nurse, Ms. Royen. It seems I was supposed to know that I should go to her office to get my TB meds. Oops. I'd actually forgotten that I'd even tested positive for that back in Delano. (Almost certainly contracted when I was first arrested and spent two hours crammed in a holding tank with about 40 others. By far the most third-world experience of my entire incarceration.)

I know that TB exposure seems like a big thing to slip one's mind, but the reaction of my skin test was so unnoticeable that I really didn't believe the med-tech was reading it right. I still don't, but Ms. Royen is so nice, I won't mind coming to see her once a week. She is concerned and professional and warm — nothing like the usual stereotype of prison medical staff.

She obviously enjoyed speaking with someone who knew a thing or two, medically speaking. So I decided to tell her about Spanky's little stunt at Cedar, the whole "don't eat after" witch-hunt based on a misinterpreted article fed to him by a guard, no less. She was pretty alarmed, even shocked.

Seizing the moment, I told her that I would really appreciate it if she could somehow get a memo sent from someone in authority to the guards at Redwood, telling all barbers (there is one for each race) that the HIV-positive inmates must be allowed access to the clippers. (Yeah, another little dilemma I didn't want to share until I'd gotten it resolved.)

I could have stopped there, but somehow it felt like I had three wishes, and this was my only chance to get them granted. So I asked that she intervene in the matter of Tefunk.

I don't know his real name. That's just what he has tattooed across his rather impressive chest. (I think it's his rap-star wannabe moniker; hip-hop being his absolute passion.) Tefunk has the bunk next to Earl, about three down and across from mine, and I'm aware of him not just because of his awesome pecs but because of a seriously hacking cough. One time Earl asked about it, and Tefunk told him he had been transferred from one of those prisons baking much farther out in the desert than this bucolic place (we have three whole trees, after all) because his cough was diagnosed as an allergy to dust. That is no damn allergy to dust, I told Ms. Royen. It is either an acute bacterial infection or tuberculosis, or perhaps even lung cancer. Nurse Royen started to tell me that Tefunk tested negative for TB, and then stopped herself. "I can't really get so specific about another patient, so pretend you didn't hear that. Let me just say that we knew there was a problem, but we thought it was getting better, not worse, so I'm really thankful you brought this to my attention. I'm going to make a special request that William gets an MRI. They really hate authorizing this stuff, but..."

William. No wonder he goes by Tefunk.

She leaned over and stage-whispered against her flat hand, "I'm going to tell them another inmate is thinking about suing over the HIV issues, and if they give in on this, I may convince him to reconsider."

"Oh, Ms. Royen you are a woman after my own heart. Sneaky for all the right reasons."

We had what one might call "a moment." I've had them all my life with women, of course, but I don't think Ms. Royen has had many with gay men. And I could tell it gave her a little kick — all to the soundtrack of the Christian radio station playing quietly on her desk. I almost thought of asking her to vote for

Kerry, but I realized that would be a fourth wish, and I really shouldn't push it.

Tefunk got a summons to the doctor that very afternoon. When he returned, he questioned Earl:

"Did you complain about my coughing?"

"No, Tefunk, I didn't."

He looked up at Adam.

"Did you?"

Adam scoffed, as if the very question was beneath him. Then Tefunk followed Earl's eyes, which were on me, of course, because Earl is constitutionally incapable of discretion or subtlety.

Tefunk walked over to me, coming into my driveway — a trespass that caused a definite ripple across the dorm.

"Man, why you have to get up in my personal business?"

I got off my bunk, so I could address him more easily in the voice I use when I want to be heard only by the person I'm talking to. (If what follows sounds rehearsed, it's because I had indeed been going over it in my head for hours, as I was afraid he might react like this.)

"This may be hard for you to believe, Tefunk, because white inmates are not supposed to give a shit about black inmates, but when another human being is coughing his lungs out every night a few beds from me, I do give a shit. It bothers me, not just because it keeps me awake, but because it sounds really painful. And if this prison can take care of me, with all the health shit I'm dealing with, they sure as fuck can take care of you."

I really didn't know how this was landing, but I was glad I'd obsessed over every word.

Tefunk leaned toward me ever so slightly, keeping his voice low just as I had kept mine.

"You know I got to front a little for the homies, right?"

"Er... I guess."

"I ain't really mad, I just gotta make like I am."

I wanted to call bullshit, to tell him he didn't have to do any such thing, that this was, in fact, a perfect example of the how the rigid rules of prison life were perpetuated by the same people who most suffered under them. I wanted to slap him across the face, like Cher in *Moonstruck,* and tell him to "snap out of it!" But I didn't, of course,.

Instead, I made a request.

"Well, can you pretend to *not* be mad, now?"

"I got something figured out."

Tefunk did a little flick of his head, like he had made his point, and then began to walk back to his bunk. He spoke as if thinking out loud; but just loud enough to be heard.

"Nigga can't get in to see a doctor to save his life, but the white boy just asks..." He shook his head, as if lamenting the way of the world.

The weird thing was that he kind of had a point.

Support came from an unexpected source, D-Roll, addressing Tefunk with a long, pointy finger.

"You could say thank you, nigga! This dude is square! He did you a solid!"

Uh-oh. This was getting way too much attention, now.

I started to open my mouth, to assure D-Roll that it was fine, *fine,* really, but Tefunk cut me off with a pulverizing coughing fit. Not his finest lyrics maybe, but definitely his most well-timed.

An hour later, a van arrived to take him to the hospital.

The Man Who Knew Too Much

When I clean the bathrooms here, I remember two things my parents taught me when I was just a teenager. My father's lesson was to never look down on manual labor, that all work has dignity. The second was from my mother. It's a French proverb, *"Ce qui mérite d'être fait, mérite d'être bien fait."* ("What deserves to be done, deserves to be well done.") So the commodes on my watch are spic n' span, and I actually take pride in the work.

By odd coincidence, the small circle of gay men I've met here from different dorms (at Pill Call every day for our HIV meds) all seem to have landed porter jobs. Supposedly, these assignments are random, but Dale (Cypress Hall) swears the administration sniffs out the gay boys for these duties. "They seem to know we're the only ones who can clean worth a shit."

Brad (Palm Hall) tossed in an apropos line from *Valley of the Dolls,* "Sparkle, Nealy, sparkle!"

Earl laughed along with us as if he understood the joke, but I had to explain the last line to him on the walk back, as his knowledge of vital gay cinematic history is sorely lacking.

Jersey, my very straight co-worker, hates cleaning the bathroom so much that he only does the butch part, which consists of running the high-powered hose on the shower floors. I shouldn't put up with this, but he is an inexhaustible compendium of information both trivial and essential about every street, drug, and prison-related topic you can think of. Our unspoken deal is that I do most of the work, but he keeps me entertained while I do it.

For example, he recently shared his Universal Theory of Addictive Hierarchy (UTAH):

"The pot-smokers look down on the pill-poppers, and the

pill-poppers look down on the coke-addicts, and the coke-addicts look down on the speed-freaks, and the speed-freaks look down on the smack-junkies. And of course, everyone looks down on the crack-heads, even other crack-heads."

"What about the alcoholics?"

"Oh, they're way up here at the top. They look down on everybody."

Jersey claims he was an intelligence officer in the Army once upon a time, before he "fucked up royally" in a manner he won't disclose. I have no trouble believing he would've had a great future there because he always seems to know the inside scoop while never revealing how he found it out.

Like last week, there was serious friction between the blacks and the Latins, leading to an unbelievably tense 20 minutes or so in the wing as both races stood by their bunks, ready to spring on each other at a moment's notice. The atmosphere was electric, like a tornado was about to hit. So we asked Jersey what was happening.

"A Paisa bumped into a Crip coming out of chow. Didn't say 'excuse me' or maybe just not fast enough. The Crip felt disrespected, and called him out. They almost went at it there, but their wingmen convinced them to take it back to the dorm." (A wingman is the inmate who has your back whenever you're together. Viper, for example, is Jersey's wingman.) Luckily, the shotcallers successfully negotiated a resolution to this *contretemps,* and everything went back to normal. I suspect, despite Jersey's authoritative account, that there was something far more serious at stake. But if he knew, he wasn't telling.

Jersey makes me miss having a computer, because I can't confirm or disprove some of his sketchier assertions, like Chino was originally a Japanese internment camp during the war; or the word *"schmutz"* is actually Yiddish for "smegma." The reason he told me this appetizing factoid is that I wondered aloud why there was always *"schmutz"* on one of the commodes every morn-

199

ing, evidently remnants of someone having thrown up. After we argued for five minutes about the true meaning of *schmutz,* he told me that one of the junkies probably gets high during the middle of the night and comes in here to toss his cookies.

I had totally forgotten that often happens to heroin users. "In fact," Jersey said, "that's what they die of when they O.D. They aspirate their own vomit."

This unpleasant tidbit did put those other tidbits in a different light. "So I should be grateful for a little bit of drek to clean up in the morning," I said, changing up my Yiddish word. "I'd rather clean up after a live junkie than a dead one, any day."

Jersey started to say something, then changed his mind.

"What?" I prodded.

"Nothing."

But there was something.

Poor Jersey. It was hard sometimes, being the man who knew everything.

Knowing how tight-lipped he could be when he wanted, I went back to cleaning. Suddenly the penny dropped. There could only be one thing he was reluctant to tell me. The junkie was Hippie.

Hippie is Earl's new bunkie. (His old bunkie, Scotty, rolled himself up to Birch rather than pay a drug debt. Nobody really liked Scotty, so we didn't care.) Hippie is so named because he used to have super-long hair until Miss Reid (back over at Cedar) made him cut it just below the ears. This sounds dictatorial and unreasonable, but they had a huge problem with his hair clogging the shower drain over there, and as the person who has to continually un-gunk ours, I'm glad he's not making my job any harder. Hippie is very resentful about it, though, and insists the real reason she made him cut it was that she was jealous. (You might remember she was the guard who changed wigs weekly.)

Hippie would be quite handsome if his head didn't have such an equine shape to it. You just want to ask, "Why the long face?"

every time you see him. But I liked him immediately because he sat with Lynn and me without a second thought his first day here, not giving a shit about the assumptions that might be drawn about him as a result. (Though nominally straight, I'm sure he has slept with men as well as women, and probably a transsexual or two as well.)

His real significant other is heroin, and has been for decades, but since his return here (on a parole violation), he seemed to be entertaining the notion of using this stay as a serious attempt at what he calls "poor man's rehab." In fact, he told me that the six weeks since he was arrested were the longest he'd been clean in memory.

Unfortunately, addiction is a pretty wily beast, and this is a tough place to stay on a pink cloud for long. Plus, Hippie seems to suffer from a fair amount of "junkie pride," which is best described as a quasi-spiritual reverence addicts develop for their relationship with heroin. The only thing it reminds me of, ironically, is the way 12-steppers speak of their sobriety. When I mentioned this to Hippie, he reacted defensively.

"I've had friends of mine get sober. And you know what, they just replace one addiction with another, with all those meetings. What's the point? You're still an addict!"

"C'mon, Hippie. Name one friend who got sober and started stealing shit, wrecking cars, or getting evicted. Name one person you know who had to go to the emergency room because he overdosed on too many meetings. All addictions aren't alike, just because they're technically addictions."

Hippie was deflated that I had punctured his steel-trap logic. (What did he think I was going to say? *"Yup, heroin... AA... NA... it's six of one, half dozen of the other."*)

Standing there with my mop in the bathroom, I realized that Hippie had stopped talking about how many days he'd gone without heroin, and that coincided with his getting some money from his mom in New York.

"Is Hippie using again?" I asked Jersey.
He shrugged, as if he didn't know, but he did.

An Oddity

We porters have a supervisor, Otis. He's an older black inmate who takes his job very seriously, although his duties consist largely of keeping a close tab on spray cleaner supplies and doling out clean rags. Since we are inspected weekly, and whichever dorm is judged cleanest gets to be first to line up for chow for the next seven days, winning this small privilege is a source of pride for Otis. It also keeps Miss Baylor off our backs. She's a young, black C.O. with a bit of a chip on her shoulder, and can be arbitrary and rude. She's not particularly bad-looking, but someone pegged her with the name "Chewbacca" for some reason, and it stuck.

Otis was a pain at first, micromanaging my particular bathroom cleaning techniques. Eventually, I snapped at him, but when we won "cleanest dorm" that week, he actually went out of his way to compliment me for a job well done. As a peace offering, I got him some rolling papers at canteen, and he was incredibly grateful. A tobacco addiction is the principle and sometimes only pleasure for many of the guys here.

So this morning Otis scurried down the wings gathering up his porters. "Get your blues on, get your blues on, there's an oddity!" "Get your blues on" just means to put on a work shirt and tuck it in, but I was stumped by the "oddity."

I asked Otis to clarify. "What did you say there was?"

"An 'oddity!' That's what Miss Baylor said. An oddity!" As he went off to fetch more porters, I heard him say under his breath, "Damn Chewbacca."

An "oddity." It's something Maggie Smith would say playing Miss Marple in an Agatha Christie mystery, "I'm afraid, Inspector, there's been an oddity."

I was the first one up to the office. The door was ajar, and

Miss Baylor was filling out some paperwork. Like a boy in the 8th grade, her left leg was pumping furiously under the desk. I had never seen that in an adult, much less a woman.

I took a step away, afraid to catch her in what seemed like a private moment, but my movement caught her attention. She came to the door.

"Can I help you *Homestead?"* she asked with a sarcastic edge, adding an "H" to my name, like most everybody.

"Otis said you wanted to see the porters."

Just then he arrived, two more in tow behind him.

"The others are on their way, Miss Baylor."

"Oh," she said, remembering that she had indeed issued that order, "Never mind. They had to reschedule the audit. Probably tomorrow. I'll let you know."

Otis stood there, momentarily confused.

"Is there a problem, Mr. Woods?" asked Miss Baylor. "I said there'll be no audit today. You are dismissed."

Otis walked with me back to my bunk, although his was in the other wing. He knew he had misunderstood, but wasn't quite sure how.

"An audit, Otis," I explained. "It's just another way to say 'inspection.'"

"Well, why don't she say 'inspection' then? I know what the fuck that is."

He suddenly realized he was in the wrong wing, and turned around.

"Goddamn Chewbacca."

Welcome to My Hood

After Hippie joined Lynn and me for chow, the (second) invisible wall that had been around us came down. Jersey and Viper sat with us a few times, and then Earl finally left Don to sit with us. But the big "get" — as they say in Hollywood — was Jimmy, who rose to shotcaller only a week or so after his return to Chino.

It is now official in Redwood Hall — eating with gay people will not give you cooties.

This coincided with another change in my circumstances. My bunkie, Steve, was paroled. Earl went immediately to Miss Baylor and asked if he could become my bunkie. We were nervous about it, because Jersey had heard her say, "they're getting a little too comfortable in here," and we were sure that could only mean us, the gays.

Whether it was Earl's obsequiousness or we just caught her on a good day, Miss Baylor approved the move. Hippie was a little bummed but seemed to understand. I mean, how could we not do this? I'll get to tell people that I was not only openly gay in prison but so was my bunkie, and it was common knowledge we were both HIV—positive, to boot. How cool is that?

It's the fact that we are just friends that is most subversive to these guys. They just don't get that we could be attracted to men, but not to each other. I don't think one of them has ever had a purely platonic friendship with a woman they are not related to. If she's willing, they'll have sex with her, regardless of how much they even really want to.

Not to say our friendship is platonic in the same way their friendships are. Straight men, especially in prison, are always jockeying for position, sniffing out if they are above or below you in the pecking order. There's none of that between Earl and me, and that lack of testosterone bullshit seems to be very attractive to Jimmy — I suppose because he tires of having to maintain his status as King of the Hill. Over here in "the gayborhood," as he calls it, he can just eat (my) crackers and drink (my) coffee and be himself.

If he is using us (well me, mostly) I don't care. If anyone had ever asked me how I thought I would ever survive prison (the kind of dinner party conversation positing a supposedly unimaginable situation), I would have almost certainly said that I'd make friends with the most powerful guy there and obtain his protection. And without much trying, that seems to have happened. If Jimmy bats his big blue eyes at me to get a couple of free soups, it's a small price to pay.

I've said this before, but it's worth repeating. Prison culture is very different depending on the security level of the facility. I think that more would be expected of me for protection in a Level II (medium) or Level III (maximum) than sharing some commissary. Although, at the ripe old age of 45, I doubt I would be someone's "punk." (Not that I would mind if I were Jimmy's, frankly.)

After a week or so of his daily visits, I decided to put this new friendship to the test.

"So listen, Jimmy I have a problem."

"I know, you have to bunk with Pearl." (Earl pretends to be offended by this moniker, but he loves any attention from Jimmy.)

"Have you noticed how long my hair is getting?"

"Not really. I thought you liked it that way."

"No, I do not like it this way. They won't let me use the clippers here. Rambo said the Latins and the blacks wouldn't agree to it."

Rambo was the previous shotcaller, who, despite his name, was not much of a fighter. In fact, he seemed more than relieved to abdicate in favor of Jimmy — who, I'm told, has an extremely mean left hook.

Jimmy didn't utter a word. He just handed me back my box of crackers (which he'd so considerately emptied), got up, and walked up to the front of the wing.

I exchanged a hopeful look with Earl. He had managed to get his hair cut when he first arrived, but had since then been frozen out, like me.

About five minutes later, I heard "Olmsted!" boom down the corridor. At the top of the wing stood Jimmy, holding the clippers and gesturing to an empty chair. Over his arm was a white towel, giving the general impression of a maître'd offering a diner a seat.

He hadn't had enough time to negotiate the use of the clippers from the other races, so must have just requested them from Miss Baylor. I suspected he'd flirted with her too, those eyelashes being easily as lethal as his fists.

Jimmy, it turns out, has been barber for the whites during several of his incarcerations (constituting most of the last 15 years). The haircut he gave me was almost as good as the one I got from Undertaker back at County, although, of course, I told Jimmy his was the best I'd ever received.

P.S. My friend Ellen sent me four books, none directly from the publisher. I dreaded dealing with Sargent Erlichson again, but this time he was completely sober and surprisingly reasonable. He could have easily sent them back, but he just handed me the box rather genially. Makes me wonder if the Chino authorities are reading the blog and reprimanded him for the last episode.

Of the books, I was particularly taken with *Three Junes* by Julia Glass. I have been completely taken out of this world and into the world she creates — in Greece, Scotland, and Manhattan in the '80s (rather a familiar time and place, that last one.) One of the books I'm reading slowly because I can't bear for it to end.

Ellen also sent me a decent dictionary, the essays of E.B. White — so good — and Bill Clinton's *My Life,* which I gladly loaned to Jimmy as a thank you for the haircut. He is very impressed that I have friends who do things like send me 900-page hardcover autobiographies.

And so am I.

Chemical Spill

The manufacture of pruno (prison wine) is a devotional art here, and I have finally pieced together how exactly it's made. Once a week, we get "real" pineapple or orange juice at breakfast and that is collected in trade for coffee or cookies. In addition, inmates collect oranges and apples that come frequently enough in lunch bags; these are peeled and squeezed for juice. A "kicker" is then added — something that triggers the fermentation process. (I don't know what kickers are made of; inmates tend to treat it as a professional secret.)

The resulting concoction is all mixed up in a plastic bag, which then goes below a bunk, in a locker or behind a toilet. Over the next few days, the chef blows into it periodically because CO_2 is necessary to the process. It takes about three or four days before it's sufficiently strong, pulled in time for a Saturday night "party" or before it gets discovered — although sometimes guards look the other way when it is. Once at Delano we had our bunks tossed while we were at Yard, and when we came back, a bag of pruno in mid-fermentation was untouched. There is no way in hell they didn't see it.

I drank a bit of pruno once at Birch, but found it an odd sensation to be tipsy here. There was nothing to "do" with the buzz, and I found myself wanting to be sober again ASAP, so I could concentrate on the book I was reading undistracted.

This reaction was a great relief to me. Before my addiction to meth took center stage, I used to drink quite heavily, and I was afraid the desire/impulse to get drunk would kick in again. (I know, I know, why tempt fate? That's a complex question that I don't have a good answer to.)

Most inmates don't bother with pruno because it's not much fun to get drunk with a bunch of other straight men when you can't then go pick up women. I don't really get why anybody would bother doing meth here, either. Both alcohol and crystal prime the pump of the libido, and horny is the last thing you want to be in this place. Even if you're willing to dip your wick with another guy, there's no place to go in a dorm. I don't even know how and when anybody jerks off. (I thought for sure I'd see that going on under the sheets in the middle of the night, but all is quiet in D-wing no matter what time I get up to take a piss.)

By far the biggest mood-alterer here is a tranquilizer named Seroquel, which is dispensed to a ridiculous proportion of the inmates — easily one in five, maybe more. It's very strong and allows you to sleep away your sentence, more or less, if you want. And if you don't want to, you can sell it to other inmates who do.

I can't really blame the Bureau of Corrections for all the over-medicating. Politicians have created this overcrowding, and there isn't nearly enough staff to deal adequately with all the mental health/substance abuse issues in the population. It's easier to just prescribe us into relative docility.

Ironically, that makes the California prison system one of the biggest drug-dealers in the world.

Last night we had a little industrial accident here, as it were. Very close to me, a neighbor was "burping" his pruno. That's the part of the homemade "winemaking" process that involves blowing into the mix. A fair amount was being made for some of the black guys to have a little party Saturday night (they call themselves "the band of brothers"). My neighbor pulled the plastic bag up and out of the industrial bucket in which it had been fermenting, and suddenly.... Schooop! The bag broke.

Several gallons of homemade pruno, replete with bits of fruit, spread in a large pond under three bunks, including mine. The holder of the bag uttered "Oh, shit...!" and his buddy added, "We're in trouble..." Everybody stared in shock and horror. The whole dorm could be denied privileges for this. And if the pruno-makers were caught, extra time on their sentence was a certain consequence.

Count had just cleared, which meant the guard on duty — Moody — was back in the guard booth. Our wing cannot be seen directly from that booth. But the nightly cleanup had already taken place, and the mops were back in the janitor's closet. Marooned on my top bunk, I finally managed to sputter out in a stage whisper, "The yellow laundry bin in the shower room, there are plenty of dirty towels in there!" (It is where I throw the cleaning rags after wiping down the bathroom.)

Little by little, towels and sheets were found to mop up the mess; a mop and a bucket were somehow produced; lockers and beds were moved and floors cleaned. During the middle of this, Moody appeared at the end of the hallway, turning a key in a circuit box as the guard on duty does every night for lights out. We held our collective breath, but somehow he did not turn and look down the wing, where he would have surely noticed several beds pulled out from the wall.

Otis got hold of some bleach and Pine Sol, which managed to kill the smell. As quietly as possible, I took the towels back into the bathroom and rinsed them out. As I walked back to my bunk, several of the black guys whispered, "thanks, man." This little misadventure was the only time I'd ever seen seamless co-operation between the races. As I drifted off to sleep, it seemed to me that the temporary solidarity had left a good feeling across the dorm.

We woke up in the morning to see a complete discoloration of the brown floor, virtually outlining the spill. This panicked me, but everybody else seemed remarkably Zen about it. They knew that assigning individual guilt at this stage would be virtually impossible.

As luck would have it, Miss Baylor called in sick, and Moody was pulling a double. He strolled down the wing for morning

Count, checking names off the clipboard, and didn't appear to notice a thing.

Or perhaps, he decided not to see what he didn't want to see.

The N-Ward

I don't think I mentioned that Rudy, the Marlboro-smuggling hottie I met in the doctor's waiting room soon after arriving at Redwood, turned out to indeed be playing for the home team. I found out when he joined Earl, Jamie and me at evening yard, and came on to Jamie pretty hard. (Yes, the same Jamie that Blue, aka Mr. Chin, had a crush on over at Cedar.) Jamie found Rudy's attentions far more to his liking, though, and I guess they had some semblance of a fling until Jamie got paroled about two weeks ago.

Since then I haven't been to Yard, but Earl goes, and last night he came back shaking.

"Rudy got jumped by a bunch of white guys."

"Oh, shit. Guys from this dorm?" I asked.

"I don't think so."

"How bad did they hurt him?"

"They tried to kick the shit out of him, but he fought back hard. I think he's okay. He walked away from it, at least."

That wasn't as odd is it sounds. Beat-downs like that are lightning quick — bam, bam, bam, and then the perpetrators take off like ghosts. By the time the guards react, it's practically over. If they'd wanted to really hurt him, they would have used a shank, or even a rock.

Still, it was very unnerving. If I'd had a shot of vodka, I would have given it to Earl to calm him down. He was stricken with the fear this was a warning to the openly gay inmates that we were getting "too comfortable," as Miss Baylor had put it.

I told him he was being melodramatic.

"Well, they called him a 'nigger-loving faggot' as they beat him up, so you tell me."

Hearing both "gg" words together, even secondhand, was a punch to the gut. But it offered a clue.

"Let's ask Jersey," I suggested. "He'll know."

"Yeah. He always knows."

Sure enough, the epithets matched the supposed crime. Jersey said Rudy had been seen leaving the lower bunk of a black inmate in the middle of the night. (They would have created privacy by hanging sheets on either side.) It seemed like an absurd risk to take, but Rudy was definitely a risk-taker.

We were perversely reassured by knowing his perceived infraction was not having sex with another man, but crossing the color line to do it. It was a horrible way to feel better, but we did. It seems that being gay, alone, will not get you beat up.

So, The "N-Ward" refers to my plan to reform the American prison system.

My idea is to segregate the population into "N" and "V." The "N" stands for "Non-Violent," and "V" for "Violent." All incoming inmates would have a choice — they could sign a pledge to be Non-Violent, and live in N-Wards with considerable privileges; or refuse to sign it and go to a V-Ward with far fewer privileges. (It's not a given that everybody would sign it; a lot of gang members might not.)

The moment that an inmate in the N-Ward does anything violent, he would be reassigned to a V-Ward. In the current system, violence is punished with extra time, which some men prefer to losing their status by refusing to fight. But what if you gained status by refusing to fight, because you were honoring your word? The notion of "honor" is actually pretty big here, for a simple reason — it's the only thing that can't be taken from you. You can be stripped of your freedom, your possessions, in some cases, your dignity, but you can always, always, keep your word.

I've been thinking about this for a while. My first idea was to have gay dorms on the state level — not just in LA or San Francisco — but I've met plenty of straight guys here who hate the violence, too. They'd love to feel that they could say "no" to using their fists without risking becoming victims themselves.

An essential part of this plan would be getting the right correctional officers in charge. Not just because they want to feel safer as they work, but also because they want their jobs to be about more than just warehousing men.

Among guards and prisoners alike, there is such an ache in here for prison to be a less desolate experience; to be, even, a meaningful one. Just imagine if men emerged from this place better people than they went in?

It's hard to understate how foreign the idea of peaceful conflict resolution is to these guys, though. Violence is so deeply ingrained in them — it's all that most of them have ever known. The other day, there was a little group clustered over in the gayborhood — Earl, Jimmy, Viper, Jersey, a guy named Dusty, me, and a new guy whose name I never caught. We were just shooting the shit about our childhoods, and Jimmy found it hard to believe that I never got spanked growing up.

"Oh, c'mon, everybody gets spanked at least once."

"You're right, there was one time... when my mother was trying to teach me to be afraid to step off the curb in front of traffic. Just one smack on the butt, that was all it took."

"Jesus, that's it?" asked Dusty, genuinely incredulous. "For your entire childhood?"

"Hand-to-God."

I can't tell you how weird the looks were on the faces around me.

I threw out a question.

"Who here got spanked growing up?"

Five hands went up.

"And who got more than spanked? Hit?"

Every hand stayed up.

"Man, I got beat all the time," said Viper.

"My mom was a slapper," added Jersey. "Sometimes a hairbrush."

"My Dad broke my arm once," said Jimmy.

Earl nodded grimly, like something similar had happened to him.

Then the nameless boy — very young, not even 20 spoke up.

"Yeah, I got smacked a lot. But you've got to understand... I deserved it... I was a *really* bad kid."

More nodding.

Then everybody fell silent for a few seconds, as if for just a moment, they understood how utterly sad that was.

The Day Chewbacca Laughed

I was hanging out with Jimmy this afternoon doing the crossword puzzle (his favorite thing to do with me), and suddenly, we heard 'wham!' We looked up to see that D-Roll had been thrown up against his locker by C-Crazy, an inmate who doesn't live in this dorm, but I've seen over here a few times visiting D-Roll. I try not to pay too much attention to any transactional activity here, but D-Roll's bunk is right next to mine, and it's been impossible not to notice C-Crazy's increasingly irritated tone of late.

He'd evidently lost patience with one too many unkept promises.

"Where are my fucking soups, D-Roll?"

As he said this, he released his grip just enough for D-Roll to slither out and scamper like a panicked crab over his bottom bunk, setting up a minute or so of slapstick maneuvering whereby C-Crazy tried to grab him from either side as D-Roll leapt to safety, back and forth over his bed.

Through all this D-Roll begged, pleaded and cajoled:

"Listen, man, something came up. I was going to come over and talk to you — man, hang on, you don't got to be so mad! — I'll get you your shit, I swear..." and so on.

He was saved by the loudspeaker announcing the end of Yard. That also means that everyone has to get back to his dorm by Count.

C-Crazy pointed as he stalked off, "This isn't over, D-Roll! You get me my shit tomorrow or you ain't gonna see the day after that!"

Jimmy and I exchanged a knowing look. We both appreciated a well-phrased threat.

As soon as his predator was out of the building, D-Roll found his courage. "Mothafucka is as crazy as his name! I owe him three damn soups, ain't no reason to try to kill my ass!"

He was right about that being a small number of soups over which to threaten bodily harm, so we strongly suspected there were a lot more than three involved.

D-roll gave us a "what-are-you-looking-at?" glare, and then retreated to his driveway. He opened his locker and pretended to do an inventory, even though the cupboard looked pretty bare.

I was grateful Jimmy was there. D-Roll wouldn't think of asking me if he could borrow money in his presence.

Jimmy had returned to the puzzle, intent on appearing blasé in spite of the commotion we'd just witnessed.

"Buenos Aires is too long for a South American capital," he noted. "But I'm sure about the 'B.'"

I suggested 'Brasilia.'

A few minutes later, Adam came in from Yard, strolling down the corridor with a definite swagger. He'd finally been convinced to play softball by Phil, who was sick of covering both shortstop and left field by himself. From the grin on Adam's face, I figured he'd hit a home run or something.

"I did it!" Adam announced. "I faced death and won!"

Even for someone as off-kilter as The Ketchup Kid, this seemed like an over-the-top reaction to winning a game.

Right behind him came Phil, shaking his head and muttering. At my bunk he stopped to point at Adam:

"That is one deranged negro!"

Ouch! Between black men here, that word is far worse than the n-word. It implies the sin of complete uncoolness.

Adam continued a fairly hysterical rant, slightly abridged here.

"That was so intense! I walked up to the edge of the abyss and I survived. Unbelievable!"

"Phil," I asked, "what the hell happened?"

"Some dude from Cypress hit a hard line-drive to left field. Ball took a weird-ass bounce and kept rolling way over to the fence, and this idiot goes to get it!"

He wasn't talking about just any fence, but THE fence. The one with a low-level of electric current running through it, topped by barbed wire. It was extremely rare for a ball to make it that far from the baseball field, but all new arrivals are told what to do if that happens, very explicitly, the first time they are taken to Yard. "If you are playing softball, and the ball somehow makes it to the fence — which it almost never does — you must stop at the base of the tower and ask, 'Boss, may I please get the ball?'" I remembered this because he'd chosen me at random to repeat it back for everyone. Then he added, "And then you wait until you hear, 'Proceed, inmate' before you get the ball." I had to repeat that back too. "And, by the way, retrieving a ball is the only reason you would ever need to go within 20 feet of the fence, am I clear?" He didn't make me repeat that, but the warning signs with skulls and crossbones were fairly effective reinforcement on their own.

Phil continued, "So the ball goes past the tower, and Adam doesn't stop. He just keeps running after it all the way to the fence! They're on the megaphone from the guard tower, 'do not proceed, inmate, do not proceed' and he still doesn't stop! Then they yell at him, 'freeze, inmate, now!' and they cock their rifles, and I'm thinking, 'Shit, they're gonna shoot this nigga!' And then he picks up the ball and he looks right up at them and says :

"I found it!" Adam interrupted. "And they've got their shot-guns pointed at me, ready to shoot! It was so rad! God I felt so ALIVE."

"See how alive you feel, jackass, when they put you in the hole for 30 days," declared Phil.

I was starting to think Adam was having a manic episode, the type that gets you put on Thorazine. Everything was exclamation points.

"They won't send me to the hole! They let me walk away! I just waved to them, and came back here! You know why? I didn't show fear! They respect that!"

Jimmy turned to Phil. "Why didn't they arrest him?"

Phil shrugged. "But I guarantee you they know who he is."

"Damn, right, they know! They will never forget me!"

From his bottom bunk, D-roll had been watching, incredulous. He stood up, and though a good foot shorter than Adam, bridged the height effectively with an inordinately long accusatory finger.

"You know what you are, *Braindead?* You're a clown! Bozo the goddamn clown! Niggas be getting shot all the time for doing nothing, and you goddamn ask for it like a stupid-ass, mothafucking clown! I wish they had shot you, you deserve to get shot!"

We were so transfixed by the drama playing out in front of us that we didn't notice Miss Baylor coming down the wing with two other officers in tow until they were upon us. One of them I recognized as Sargent Clavin from Cedar, so perhaps the reason Adam hadn't been arrested was because they were short-staffed and had to fetch an officer.

"Stand down, Mr. Dawkins," ordered Miss Baylor.

Hearing his last name, D-Roll turned around. Oh, shit. He'd just threatened another inmate in front of witnesses, basically. But they weren't here for him.

Clavin addressed the officer next to him, pointing at Adam. "Is this the one?"

"Sure is," uttered the guard.

"They here for me?" Adam asked.

"What do you think, Mr. Braintree?" asked Miss Baylor.

"Piece of cake," responded Adam. "Worth every minute."

He turned his back and offered his wrists for cuffing. As they led him away, all he had to say was:

"If I don't come back, you can have my ketchup, Olmsted!"

Count was called minutes later. During Count, you lie on

your stomach on your bunk and put your hands on the railing of the bed. Everyone is supposed to be silent, but out of the corner of his mouth, Phil whispered:

"Hey, Mark, you gonna share Adam's ketchup?"

I grinned, but didn't answer, because it was Count.

His second request was in the voice of a junkie jonesing for a fix.

"Please, Mark, do me a solid, I need some ketchup, man."

Because everyone was quiet, the entire wing could hear him, and they'd almost all seen what had happened earlier, of course.

I couldn't help it. I whispered back.

"No way! Get your own fucking ketchup!"

I could barely get that out without laughing, and of course, nothing makes you laugh more than trying not to laugh. Phil started laughing, and Earl started laughing, and the laughter spread contagiously. Even the few guys at the end of the wing who didn't know what had happened started laughing.

All through this, I was waiting for Miss Baylor to rap her nightstick on one of the bedframes to shut us up, which is pretty effective, especially if she chooses your bed. I finally lifted my head up to check, and there she was, clipboard in hand, bent over from laughing so hard.

Slowly, the eruption subsided, but Miss Baylor was still having trouble keeping it together. She tried to continue with the count but her laughter just started the general laughter back up again. Finally, she gave up and with some difficulty, sputtered out, "All you mothafuckas are present and accounted for."

We all sat up and started hi-fiving each other, black, white, Latino, no matter.

Miss Baylor walked back up the wing to the office, greeting someone at the end of the hallway, standing there with a duffel bag.

"Well, Tefunk, good to see you! Are you feeling better?"

"Yes, Miss Baylor, much better."

"Good to hear. We kept your old bunk open for you."

"Thanks, Miss Baylor."

She walked back to the guard booth, still chuckling to herself. "Ketchup..."

Tefunk came down to his bunk.

"Damn, I ain't never seen Miss Baylor in a good mood like that before."

P.S. When we went to chow, someone stayed behind. When we got back, he was gone. D-Roll had rolled himself up.

We've Got Female

I completely forgot to mention that Lynn left over a week ago. She was only doing 90 days for violating probation (after failing three drug tests in a row, I think) and that was cut in half because of overcrowding. We shared a goodbye cookie the night before she left, but didn't make any pretense that some life-long friendship had been made.

I did ask her one thing during our final walk to chow.

"So, Lynn, what was your name as a man?"

She took her time answering, but did.

"Melvin."

I had to bite my lip, to be honest. Thank God she let out one of her trademark cackles.

"Ha! Pretty funny, isn't it?"

"Not really," I lied.

Today, Earl got a letter from her.

I am higher than a kite and loving it! I got all dolled up in my sexiest latex brassiere, and let one of my regulars know I've returned! Man, those button-down husbands just love it when I tie them up and whip them till they cry like babies! Made $300! Woo-hoo! Lynn is back!

Earl deadpanned, "Should I share this with Miss Baylor? I think she would enjoy it."

I can't decide whose life I'd like less to see ten years from now, Lynn's or Adam's.

New Jimmy

In the six weeks or so since I've known him, getting my approval seems to have become increasingly important to Jimmy. I didn't realize this until about a week ago, when he told me about a "genius" babysitting technique he'd discovered when his old girlfriend, Amber, had asked him to look after her two rowdy boys while she was at work. "I told them that if they didn't start behaving, I'd beat their mom when she got home. Worked like a charm!"

He told me this with a sort of perverse pride, evidently thinking that I would approve of his creativity in child-rearing methods. I was horrified, of course,.

"I wouldn't have really beat her," he insisted defensively.

"But they didn't know that!"

"Exactly!"

I imagine the same threat had been used on him when he was a child, and he even remembered it as one of the kinder disciplinary methods he'd received from a series of temporary stepfathers. But that didn't make it okay.

"You really can't see what a terrible thing that is to say to a kid?"

I think it was seriously the first time it had dawned on him.

My reproach really upset him. The next morning, he told me he couldn't sleep the night before because of my reaction. And that he wanted to tell me something.

"That same girl, Amber, she was getting stalked by her ex. Making her life miserable. One night, he drove up, and I sent her and the kids out the back. I left the door unlocked, and waited in the dark. And when he came in, I hit him with a pillowcase full of batteries. *Wham! Wham!* Then I dragged him back out to his car, punching and kicking him the whole way. Threw him behind the wheel, and told him if he ever bothered her again, I would kill him."

"Jeez, Jimmy. What if he had a gun?"

He shrugged, as if the possibility had never even crossed his mind.

I had no idea how true any of this was, but that didn't really matter. He'd wanted to redeem himself in my eyes, to show me he could be violent for a noble purpose. In that sense, it worked. I gave him back his "good guy" status.

Tonight, I was walking back from chow with him, and a young guy with a tattoo reading "Casey" on his neck stopped to ask him a question.

"Hey, Jimmy, if someone said, 'gimme a light, punk!' to you, you'd clip him, right?"

It was like he and his homies had been having an argument and wanted Jimmy to settle it.

"Depends," said Jimmy. "Are you a punk?"

"Hell, no!" answered Casey.

"Then don't give him a light," said Jimmy, getting a laugh and good exit line.

I started walking, and he caught up with me.

"Man, don't do that!"

"Do what?"

"Abandon me!"

"What are you talking about? I waited for you."

"Like, way over in East Buttfuck!"

This was clearly an exaggeration, considering I was near enough to hear their exchange. What he meant was that I had been standing at the distance of that nerdy neighbor kid who the cool jock sometimes walks with home from school, but who doesn't know whether he has the social status to stand close by when the cool jock stops to talk to the other cool jocks.

"You know what," I told Jimmy when we got back to the

dorm, "I'm leaving in a week. Don't you think it's a little late to start asking me to be your wingman?"

"Why not?" asked Jimmy. "I have your back."

"Number one, those guys weren't about to jump you. Number two, if they did jump you, it would probably be because I stood too close to you. South Buttfuck instead of East Buttfuck."

I jutted my pelvis forward, grabbing onto imaginary hips.

Jimmy grinned. "Like you would ever be on top."

"Maybe not, but don't you think Casey's question was a little fishy? You're walking with an openly gay prisoner and he asks about being called a 'punk?'"

"Probably. Maybe I should've clocked him. But that's 'Old Jimmy.' 'New Jimmy' uses his words."

"That was good, by the way." I repeated his line back to him, but as Mae West would deliver it, " *Then don't give him a light,*" I growled as she would growl.

Jimmy laughed, but I had to explain it to Earl.

A big black guy named Bear has moved into D-Roll's former bunk. He's incredibly soft-spoken and gentle, and asked me to find him a pen-pal when I get out.

After this conversation, Jimmy went back to his wing. Bear and I were stretched out on our bunks, waiting for count. Bear said to me:

"That Jimmy guy?"

"Yeah?"

"He *likes* you."

And Then There's Leo's Dad

Phil left this morning, and I got way more of a farewell from him than Sharif did. In fact, he opened up to me for a good hour last night about his anxieties related to getting out.

He is paroling to his sister's place, but she is a devout Jehovah's Witness and drives him absolutely nuts with her proselytizing. He's fatalistically certain that within a week, he'll run into some of his old buddies and they'll invite him over for some "chronic" and cognac, and he'll be off to the races again, selling enough dope to get by — but not enough to make any "real" money. He put it this way,

"Let me tell you, you've got to be a ruthless motherfucka to make it selling drugs in my neighborhood, and that ain't me. You ain't gonna believe this, but I used to carry a *toy* gun. They didn't even want me in their gang! Brothers said, 'Phil, you too much of a damn pussy to be bangin.' "

I thought this was hysterical. "I bet they kept you around anyway, just for the company."

"Naw, you're the only one who thinks I'm funny. You and my ex-wife."

He smiled at a private memory.

"That was a good time. I had an okay job, too."

"What was that?"

"Repairing Xerox machines."

"What happened with that?"

"Got all computerized and shit. I couldn't keep up. My dys— what'd you call it again?"

"Dyslexia."

"Yeah, that."

He was quiet for a while. More memories.

"I got a son, you know."

"Really? How old?"

"Seven. He turned seven the day before yesterday."

"Are you going to see him?"

"I don't know. It's all complicated with his mom. She never forgave me for getting arrested and I don't blame her. She met another guy — that's who Leo calls his dad. I don't want to confuse him."

For once, Mr. Advice over here was hoping he wasn't going to ask for any. What the fuck did I understand about growing up in Compton, anyway, with the corner church and the street corner the only choices that seem open to you?

Evidently, just enough.

"What should I do, Mark?"

Oh, geez.

There was a scene in *Maude* when her maid, Florida, is leaving, and Maude says, "This isn't goodbye! Between Walter and me going to visit you, and you and James coming over here..." Then she trails off because she realizes that's a bunch of bullshit, and they'll never see each other again.

So I didn't pretend to Phil that we would get in touch. But I did make two suggestions.

"I've actually never been on parole, Phil, but I think you should make your P.O. earn his or her paycheck. I know there are a lot of re-entry programs that both the state and foundations pay for, and it seems like I've read tons of articles about how hard it is to find enough motivated ex-cons to stick with them. So... I don't know, maybe you can get hooked up into one of those. I'd sure take a chance on you. I mean the one thing you think of as your biggest weakness might actually be your greatest strength."

"What's that?"

"That you're *not* ruthless. People want to hire a nice guy a lot more than they want to hire a scary guy."

"I guess that's true."

"I don't know what to tell you about Leo. But if you do have a relationship with him eventually, I think you'll be good at it. 'Cause you *are* a really nice guy. And that's the most important thing a father can be, by far."

I told him a little about my own heroically kind dad. Unlike the dyslexia story, every word was true.

When he left, Phil actually gave me a hug, which is pretty unheard of here, but considering I only have three days left and I'm in this weird platonic relationship with the King of the Woods, if anyone doesn't like me getting hugged by a black guy, they can take it up with Jimmy.

P.S. I came back to my bunk and Sharif was just opening up a package he'd picked up from R&R. A book — *Protocols of the Elders of Zion.*

Oh, brother.

Before and After

I am writing this while sitting in Re-Entry Class, which reminds me a little of Health Sciences back in 8th grade — innocuous and interminable. The instructor is a well-meaning and earnest man, but "preparing" this population for a life on the outside in two mornings and an afternoon is an impossible task that would defeat Deepak Chopra. To add insult to injury, the ten-minute video that we were shown was clearly made by the nephew of some assistant warden as his filmmaking project at a local community college back around 1989. Pedantic and amateurish and just plain embarrassing. A randomly-picked episode of *Oprah* would have been more constructive.

It's all such a stupid waste. I was reading an article in the *Los Angeles Times* about the overcrowding in the state prisons. Do you realize that Germany has twice the population of California and a third of the inmates? And the things we could actually "do" with such a (literally) captive audience! It's not even a mystery how! Norway does a damn good job, and that can't possibly be more expensive than this. Someone like Phil, for example, should have left here with a degree in early childhood education. He would make an excellent elementary school teacher. Instead, he's going to get some janitorial job — if he's lucky — and will probably still end up back here, costing the taxpayers $20,000 a year.

My friend Chris is going to be picking me up at the gate Wednesday morning. We have a tortured past. I fell in love with him in 1998 when he was my drug dealer. He eventually went to prison, and I wrote to him every day for 18 months, all while I was getting sucked into the very life he had left behind. You would have thought I would have learned from his mistakes, wouldn't you? (Oh, Tina, what a treacherous drug art thou.)

Chris was released and got his life back together. But he kept his distance from me for good reason. Three years later, he found out through the grapevine that I was in here and started to write to me. This strange circle will finally complete itself when he picks me up on the day after tomorrow. I'm very grateful it'll be someone who knows exactly what it's like to be in here, and then out of here.

When I started counting down the days to my release, I began to play with the math of it all. If I live to be 80, I will have been on this earth 960 months, and so my time inside — 9 ½ months — will come to almost exactly 1% of my entire life. That number helped me gain perspective during some of the worst moments here, which, for all my fears, didn't turn out to be near the nightmare it could have been. That said, my life will always be divided in two by this experience — before and after.

Chris will be taking me to my dear friend Andrea's apartment. She is living with her fiancé at present, and so I will be able to sublet until I get a place of my own. I'll also be going to 12-step meetings and I suspect will be reconstructing an entirely fresh social network from that. I even dare hope to land a husband, perhaps even an unambiguously gay one. Imagine that!

Adieu, Boys

Wow, I get out tomorrow morning. It's hard to convey the mixture of anticipation and fear that entails. (Jeez, can you imagine what it's like for people who do *real* time? As much as I hate these walls, I can grasp how it could be a source of incredible anxiety to not have them to lean on any more.)

I had a "last meal" with Earl and Jimmy, and then said my official goodbyes to them just before evening Count. (I will be roused at 5:30 — they will both still be asleep.) Even though I've spilled a lot more ink about Jimmy recently, Earl has still been the strongest and most important relationship I've had behind bars. I acknowledged that to him tonight, and he basically said the same thing back to me, but we didn't get all teary or anything over it. I gave him my Walkman and most everything in my locker, so that helped soften the blow. And I will write to him.

When I said goodbye to Jimmy, he said he had a nice surprise for me. It seems that a few weeks back, when we first talked about his ex-girlfriend Amber, he decided to see if he could track her down through his sister. And just today, he got a letter from her! She says she's often thought about him over the years and was very happy to hear from him. Is that not cool or what?

I'm trying not to embark on too many fantasies on Jimmy's behalf, but even if all that came out of Amber's letter was the little glimmer of hope I saw in his eyes tonight, that would be a lot.

I gave him the big fat dictionary Ellen sent me — he's been eyeing that from the day I got it. "A gift of words from he who is gifted with words," said Jimmy.

He may have said something else extremely touching as he hugged me goodbye. But for once, I'm not sharing.

The Fate of Ping

My mother is terribly afraid of heights, but as children we never knew it. She would grit her teeth and wave as her brood madly ascended trees and climbed to other death-defying heights. One such occurrence was captured by a photograph taken at the very top of an aqueduct in the south of France — le Pont du Gard. In the photo there is no evidence that we children are supported by any structure whatsoever. All that can be seen behind us is the sky and the la Vallée du Gardon, stretching vertiginously in the background.

We also never knew my mother had a terrific phobia of having her head below water, even after my father put an aboveground pool in our backyard in 1964. It seems odd now that we never noticed that she kept her neck above the water. As swimming was the only sport my otherwise nonathletic father enjoyed, we were perhaps too busy getting rambunctious with him. Mostly, my mom made sure we didn't swim for a half an hour after eating. (The danger of this has since been reported as a myth, but I will believe it on my deathbed.)

In 1962, friends of my parents went off to spend a year in Europe and let us housesit for the time they were gone, rent-free. They owned a dramatic house that aspired to a Frank Lloyd Wright look and succeeded admirably. It was at the edge of a forest remnant in the hills of Montgomery County, not far from Washington D.C., amidst the kind of semi-rural sprawl where puppies were born at neighbors' houses and brought home by kids before Mom and Dad could say no. From somewhere or another we adopted a pair of beagle mixes, whom we named Ruffy and Tuffy. Or perhaps they adopted us. They were the first in a series of dogs my mother tolerated solely as an act of maternal love for us. She didn't dislike them; she'd just had no experience with them growing up, and a pet seemed more burdensome to her than anything else. I always found it curious that she could be so addicted to the all-encompassing adoration of her children yet feel relatively immune to the same devotion from a dog.

Ruffy and Tuffy were emotionally promiscuous; they may even have been increasing their caloric intake by pretending to belong as well to other families on the far side of the woods. At least that seemed the least painful explanation for their disappearance soon before we were due to move. A few miles away, at our new house on West Ritchie Parkway, we came into a black cocker spaniel mix named Zorro, no doubt named by my brother Luke, who loved sweeping around in a black cape pretend-slashing Z's on everything. No one can recollect the reason or manner of Zorro's departure from the scene, but when we met the Sagan family, we kids were agitating for a new dog.

Ginetta Sagan was short and fiery, an Italian Edith Piaf with a story as dramatic as one would imagine for a woman who would later become a well-known human rights activist. My mother might have been the first kindred spirit she met in American suburbia, a European who had been a teenage girl under the Nazi Occupation.

One afternoon, my mother and Ginetta had just finished a French-style summer lunch al fresco, and excused the children from the table to talk as they shared the fruit and cheese. I suppose I played with the other kids for a while, then drifted back to the screen door in the kitchen, the one that looked out on the deck.

The image that I return to in my head is that of Ginetta crying, her arms splayed on the table, her head pitched forward on her hands. My mother told me later that Ginetta had just recounted the story of her work in the Italian and French resistance, the murder of her parents, her harrowing capture and torture by the Nazis, and finally her near-death escape from them. My mother sat quietly across from her, tears streaming down her face, but said nothing. Some events defy consolation. An American would more likely have thought an appropriate reaction would be to make Ginetta "feel better," but my mother knew such a response would have been a form of editing, an attempt to corral the pain instead of respecting it.

Suddenly, plop! Into Ginetta's lap jumped her Pekingese dog, which she'd brought over along with her children. The dog did what dogs do so well, remind you that there is always unconditional love to be had. The dog licked her hand, gently bringing her back into the present moment. My mother handed her friend a Kleenex, and the tension was broken.

Dr. Sagan, Ginetta's husband, had told me that Pekingese once had very long noses, but had been made to compete by a Chinese Emperor in a great race. According to the legend, one of them was so fast he could not stop at the finish line and rammed into the Great Wall of China, shmushing his long nose into the form we knew ever since, and becoming progenitor of all future Pekingese.

The story delighted me as I could easily repeat it. Dr. Sagan knew how to talk to kids, and he had three handsome boys who were so much cooler than we would ever be. The Sagans lived in a huge old Victorian in the center of Rockville, which I would check at great length for secret panels when we visited. I never found one, but they were very tolerant of my knocking against every wall of the house. (This was the era of Dark Shadows; I'm afraid I took the production design quite to heart.)

Dr. Sagan was a psychiatrist, and my mother asked him to see me informally when I complained of severe headaches. I suppose she was a bit suspicious because they seemed to occur exclusively on Sundays. The headaches were quite real, but it didn't take long for the doctor to figure out that I simply had a bad case of the Catholic Church. I don't think I objected to the theology. I was just hopelessly bored, and for me that was a mortal sin.

I was dispensed from going to church for at least a few Sundays, but my headaches ended up coinciding with my mother's alienation from St. Mary's, the very traditional local parish. She was finding the U.S. involvement in Vietnam increasingly objectionable, and the church's refusal to condemn it even worse. She heard about a new place to worship, an anti-war service led by Father Richard McSorley, a Jesuit priest and theology professor at Georgetown who was a personal confidant to the Kennedy family. My headaches didn't return when we started going. But even with the cool guitar music and bell-bottomed parishioners, I was still bored. My little sister and I would often slip out of the chapel and walk around campus, imagining ourselves hip and angry college students. When The Exorcist was filmed there a few years later, we recognized every building and stairwell.

Eventually, the Sagan's Pekingese got pregnant, and we were offered one of the puppies. We named her Puff, and couldn't have been more in love. Like most small dogs, she didn't know she was small, and was extremely athletic for a Pekingese, not yappy at all. She even grew on my mother. Puff was the first of our dogs small enough to snooze on my mother's lap while she watched TV and knit, and, of course, Puff was drawn to the one who fed her.

It seems odd now, but at the time, scooping up after your dog was not a common practice. The Walls were our next door neighbors, a couple in their '70s. They were one of the few retired and childless couples on the street and as such, stood slightly apart. Certainly their devotion to their pristine lawn was singular. We learned to rush Puff past it, because any dog-do would result in an officious phone call asking for its removal. Mrs. Wall didn't seem to have much to do but look out of the window. This extended to the second floor, as she witnessed my parents' risqué skinny dipping late one night, over the cedar fence my father had put up. Dottie Sewell across the street gave us the heads up. My parents thought it terribly funny and just a bit sad, but if Mrs. Wall wanted a show, they didn't really mind giving her one.

For the first time, our canine companion was not an all-purpose mutt. Puff had papers! Our neighbor, Mrs. Simmons, who bred championship pugs for competition, encouraged us to breed Puff when she came of age. My parents didn't give a hoot about such things, thought of it as an excellent way to teach their children the facts of life.

Somehow a stud was found, and a date set in our cellar. Pekingese tend toward small litters, and the agreement was that we'd keep one puppy, the family of the male would keep one, and we'd sell or give away any others. Coitus was successful to a fault, and we had to call Mrs. Simmons and ask how to get the pair apart. My poor mother spent a good hour massaging Puff and her paramour till they unstuck. I guess we kids were supposed to understand that this had something to do with how humans made babies, but I sure didn't make the connection.

When Puff gave birth to three offspring, my parents assumed that the Super-8 film graphically documenting their egress would clear up any remaining questions we had about the birds and the bees. As if kids care about that part of the process. I ended exactly where I'd started, with a perfect understanding of vaginal birth but only the vaguest notions about arousal, insertion and ejaculation. (I had to learn all that the traditional way, through innuendo and misinformation from the friends of my older siblings, and some inappropriate touching in the Boy Scouts.)

We named the two male puppies Ming and Ling, and the third, a female, Ping. Immediately we noticed that the boys were suckling, and Ping was trying, but was being pushed away by Puff, who knew before we did that something was wrong with her. Mrs. Simmons referred us to her vet, and he made a quick diagnosis that there was an obstruction in Ping's throat.

The doctor held out a small hope that hand feeding might work; probably more to placate us than because he believed it. My mother tried for three days, watching poor Ping suckle desperately on a tiny bottle, but nothing seemed to be going down.

There was nothing else to do but watch her die.

The entire situation was unacceptable to me. Lapsed Catholic that I was, (the rock-and-roll service at Georgetown notwithstanding) God was already on thin ice with me. On the Sundays I hadn't gone to church, I'd perused the New York Times with my father. I knew about the starving children in Biafra and the My Lai Massacre. I could see plain as day the world was full of violence and suffering, and I objected. Seeing this poor little creature was the last straw. I decided then and there that if there was a God, he was either too cruel or too powerless to be worthy of worship. How could he possibly allow a puppy to be born just to starve to death? And what was this "he" pronoun, anyway? How could a formless, all-powerful, universal God even have a sex? (This was way before "gender" was the preferred term.)

Two days later, I came home from school to find my mother with tears streaming down her face. Ping had died — but my mother was not crying because of that. She was crying, she told me, because she hadn't been brave enough to drown Ping, to put her out of her misery. My mother had run up against that most unpleasant of paradoxes — sometimes the cruelest choice and the kindest choice are one in the same.

We buried Ping in the backyard, gave Ling to her father's family, and kept Ming. A year or so later, Puff got something in her eye, a common issue with Pekingese. We could not cure the infection, and had to have her eye removed. Soon after, Puff went a little crazy, treating our hamsters like her puppies. We were lucky to find a home for her when we moved to New York, taking Ming with us.

Then we took Ming camping on Cape Cod, and he got some sand in his eye. It too became infected. My mother assiduously applied an antibiotic gel, and just as the infection seemed to be clearing up, she took Ming for a walk. There was a hassle with another dog, and Ming's eye was reinjured. It would have to be taken out as well. At the time, $200 was a lot of money to spend on a dog, and no one wanted to see our beloved Ming banging into furniture like his mother. Ming was put to sleep, and my Mom was through with dogs for 40 years.

When my little sister Erica pined for some kind of pet, we decided to try a cat. We called her Minet, which is French for "kitten." Every evening Minet would be let out to roam the neighborhood, and in the middle of the night she'd wake me up with a "meow" at my bedroom door, which was downstairs. I would let her in and all was right with the world.

Then one night, she was not at the door. We searched the neighborhood with a bowl of kibbles, shaking it to attract her. But she was nowhere to be found.

AFTERWORDS

Trash Whisperer

Six months after my release, I accomplished a cherished goal. I got my dog back.

I had adopted Gaza in 1998, after he was rescued from one of those canyons north of L.A with a muzzle still attached. He didn't seem to have been otherwise mistreated, though. He had no fear of people, was housebroken and affectionate. The woman who discovered him had two dogs and three children and just couldn't keep him. She placed a small, free-to-a-good-home ad in the *Los Angeles Times* and I answered it. So commenced my 14-year love affair with this handsome pointer-mix with a marvelously sweet disposition.

The day after "Fred" (the temporary name his rescuer gave him) entered my life, I celebrated Thanksgiving at the house of a Palestinian friend. Someone there suggested "Gaza" as his permanent name, and it stuck. It appealed to me that I would never likely run into another dog with the same name, and I never did. His other memorable quirk was an extraordinary herding instinct. If another dog were chasing a ball, Gaza would stay close to it like an NBA point guard. Sometimes other dog-owners found this irritating. But mostly they were amused and it served as an endless topic of dog park small talk.

I had just left a job as an editor of a national gay men's magazine. I'd had pneumonia twice while working there, and that was enough to get me back on HIV-related disability. The cocktails were quite new and the death rate was still high, which made it easy to turn my life insurance into a lucrative viatical settlement. I had too much free time and a fat bank account, and it was easy to rationalize partying to my heart's content. After all, the actuaries had just certified that I likely had less than 24 months to live.

In the context of my predicted lifespan, it was certainly irresponsible to get a dog, but that reflected the strange dichotomy I'd always experienced around the disease. Even though I would have told you that I expected to die soon, at some deep, internal level, it didn't feel true to me. This was a dicey combination, as it fed a very cavalier sense of risk. I could use my assumed impending death as an all-purpose excuse to do what I wanted to do anyway, while actually feeling inside that I wasn't *really* endangering my health in a relentless pursuit of hedonism.

Another way I convinced myself that my increasing drug use was not slowly derailing my life was to avoid egregiously stereotypical addict behavior. My refrigerator was never empty, I called my mother regularly, and I never missed a doctor's appointment. But what most set me apart, in my mind, was how assiduously I took care of the dog. He was always well-fed, taken to the vet for shots, and almost without fail, went on a hike every day. When I was pressed for time, a few of my regular customers were happy to take him out in exchange for a free baggie.

Later on, in 12-step meetings, I often heard about someone who finally got clean when he realized how badly he was neglecting his pet. It was exactly the opposite with me. Gaza was the marker that convinced me I was handling everything just fine.

After I was sentenced to prison, my brother Steve agreed to take the dog to his house in Salinas. When I was released and finally able to bring Gaza to my new studio apartment in Hollywood, I considered it sobriety's most tangible reward so far.

The other rewards could be elusive. Although I attended 12-step meetings daily and embraced the incredible friendships to be found within the rooms, I struggled mightily with anxiety and insomnia. I also discovered that my prison record created a serious barrier to finding a decent full-time job. Thankfully I was able to cobble together a side income editing film subtitles, work for which I was ideally suited. There just wasn't enough of it.

Even though Gaza's unconditional love was always there for the taking, his capacity to receive mine with such grace was his most constant lesson. After all of the damage I'd done, it was easy to wallow in a sense of shame and regret. Gaza's inability to experience self-pity reminded me to just get over it.

There were riots at Chino a year or so after I left, and I pitched an "insider" series about my time there that served as my entré to the *Huffington Post*. My first columns discussed prison, but I ended up writing almost weekly on a wide range of political and social issues. It paid nothing, but was not without its rewards, status-wise. Among friends, I wryly paraphrased Celeste Holm in *All About Eve,* "A Huffpost blogger? I'm the lowest form of celebrity." (In the movie, she's discussing being a playwright's wife.)

My apartment was small, so I walked Gaza often and long. Given the city's perfect weather, this should have been pure delight. But Little Armenia is one of the most litter-strewn neighborhoods in the city. This infuriated me so much that I literally had to recite a well-known prayer to calm down, "God grant me the serenity to accept the things I cannot change; to change the things that I can; and the wisdom to know the difference." What could qualify more as a problem that I simply had to accept than the fact that people littered? I mean, what was I going to do? *Pick it up?*

That turned out to be my seminal moment — the thought I simply couldn't shake. Why, exactly, *couldn't* I pick it up? There was no reason, of course, at least if you didn't count the inchoate sense of dread that arose in me when I considered it seriously.

The irrationality of my resistance bothered me almost as much as the litter, so I overruled my emotional response and decided to make a test run. I bought a reaching device from the hardware store, stuffed some plastic grocery bags in my pocket, and put the leash on Gaza.

Wrappers, cups, soda cans, endless fast food packaging — my visual apprehension of the problem had not remotely done it justice. I filled my first bag before reaching the corner, but was happy to confirm what I had suspected — if you picked up trash while you were walking the dog anyway, the extra work was minimal, even fun. It was like the chore your Mom made into a game when you were a kid, "I bet you can't make your bed faster than your sister!" If a cluster of cab drivers hadn't been smoking cigarettes in front of the building next to mine, I would have completely forgotten that I had been initially reluctant to undertake this task at all.

I'd noticed them since I'd moved to the neighborhood; either sharing a smoke in the morning, before their long shift behind the wheel, or decompressing afterward — sometimes passing a flask between them. We hadn't paid much attention to each other before, but as I came close, they couldn't help but notice that I was picking up the very same empty cigarette pack that one of them had tossed just a few minutes earlier. They fell silent as I plucked it off the sidewalk, and I could feel their collective gaze follow me as I crossed the street to clean the other side.

This was exactly what I'd been nervous about; that those I caught in the act of littering would be pissed at me for catching them in the act of littering. It was similar to the fear I felt the first time I mopped C-wing; that I'd see something I shouldn't see, and it would be my fault for not having averted my eyes fast enough.

I didn't have much choice but to be afraid in prison, but damned if I was going to be afraid now. Of what, anyway? Their glares? Of them thinking I was a do-gooder, a nag, a homo?

Fuck that shit.

I liked the way the street looked clean.

End of story.

Litterbug taxi drivers weren't alone in looking sideways at me. Others assumed I collected cans for a living or was a mentally ill hoarder. At first, I wanted to explain, to point to my clear eyes and expensive glasses, to my well-nourished dog with the unmatted hair. Then gradually, another thought displaced that one.

So what? So what if they thought I was poor or schizophrenic or both? What if I just completely allowed them to draw whatever conclusions they drew, however inaccurate or mean-spirited?

I knew the Al-Anon slogan, "What you think of me is none of my business." But now its meaning sunk in. It meant letting go of the impulse to control others' perceptions of me, to instead define myself by what I knew to be true. By refusing to play the fool's game of constantly seeking validation, I could just focus on doing the next right thing.

It was a much simpler way to live, and so much less exhausting.

Of course, most people who saw me trash-picking figured out pretty fast what I was trying to accomplish and did not eye me suspiciously. You couldn't miss me — every morning for eight years I cleaned the four blocks around my apartment, unless I was sick or out of town. And every morning I got pissed off again; because without fail, there was enough new litter to fill at least two fresh bags, sometimes more.

Every day I consciously chose to put myself back into the same situation I knew would infuriate me. And every day I renewed my commitment to not only clean the street but to release my anger, one piece of trash at a time. Pluck, sigh, breathe. Pluck, sigh, breathe.

The mantra worked more days than not. Certainly, it was more efficient than any meditation I'd ever tried in producing a semblance of actual serenity.

I renamed the blog *The Trash Whisperer* because every day something happened that was worth writing about. I found angrily scrawled notes ripped from under windshield wipers, tearful apologies that had slipped out of recycle bins. I picked up love letters so sweet that it broke my heart to imagine they had been thrown away. When someone dumped a month's worth of schoolwork on the sidewalk, I furiously googled the name of the girl on the assignments, hoping to send an indignant email to her Facebook account. What I found instead was a memorial page grieving her recent death in a hit-and-run accident. (I dragged the boxes to a dumpster myself.)

There were accidental juxtapositions of discarded furniture, creating impromptu dioramas that I captured with my phone and posted online. I witnessed performance art of a kind, as well. I would have sworn, in fact, that one block of Western Avenue hosted more public breakups than any other in the city of Los Angeles. Another block seemed to materialize one new stray dog a week. I would return home with Gaza, then run back out with the leash and some treats, but I could never find them again.

Every other day or so, someone would come up to me with the same question.

"What kind of dog is that?"

I would answer, but they wouldn't really listen, as the inquiry was just an excuse to tell me about their own dog. After a few minutes I wished Gaza wasn't so unfailingly patient, and would pull me along when I gave him some sort of secret command.

Other days — most days, really — someone would say something kind and supportive about my cleaning up. By far, the very best moment occurred when a young lady in nurse's scrubs stopped me on the way to her Metro stop.

"Can I ask you your name?"

"Mark. And this is Gaza."

"What a pretty dog."

It was kind of a shame he had a gay dad, because Gaza absolutely loved women, and drew them to us constantly.

"Well, Mark, I work at Kaiser, and I've been watching you do this for a couple of months. But I'm transferring to another hospital, and I was afraid I'd never get a chance to tell you this thing I've been wanting to tell you."

I smiled. "And what's that?"

"You *inspire* me."

I discovered that homeless people truly appreciate when you ask them their names — it's a terrible thing to be invisible all the time. And some people I thought were homeless turned out to not be homeless at all. One of them, a Congolese woman who collected cans in front of my house every week, became my cleaning lady. When Gaza died, Louise cried as much as I did.

One day I was about to cross the street, and one of the members of the morning kabdriving kaffee klatch stopped his taxi next to me. He motioned me over.

"My friend, can I ask you why do you do this? Does someone pay you?"

"Of course, no one pays me!" I answered, somewhat indignantly. "I do it because I hate the way the litter looks, why else would I do it?"

He shrugged, skeptical. Still, I was happy to have the opening to finally ask the question I had wanted to ask from the beginning.

"And, sir, why do you litter?"

He seemed almost irritated that I would ask a question whose answer was so self-evident.

"The city will pick it up!"

I like to think of myself as even-tempered, but I can go from zero to 60 in no time flat, and I did.

"Oh right, if you happen to throw it right where the street-sweepers come! I've seen you litter on the sidewalk, right next to a dumpster! Is the city going to pick that up too?"

"The gardeners will clean it up."

It was true that once a month gardeners came and cleaned around and in front of most buildings in L.A. Otherwise, the city would have been buried in trash long ago. But that was a stupid excuse for sheer laziness.

"So for two, three weeks, the crap just sits there, making the block look trashy and ugly, all because you can't bother to walk three feet to throw it out!" *All because it makes you feel like a big shot to have people clean up after you,* is what I thought, but it felt like too intimate an accusation to voice out loud.

I was very close to completely losing my cool, and consciously dialed it down.

"Listen, I don't really understand why anyone would litter, but you see me picking up trash every day, and just out of respect for my efforts, I'd really appreciate it if you just didn't do it. It would just be a nice thing."

From him, another half-shrug; the closest thing I would get to assent.

You take what you can get.

Love and Memory

In August of 2011, I kept hearing an ad on the local NPR radio station promoting the Graduate program in the Humanities at Mount St. Mary's University. I had considered going back to school several times before, but could never justify going deeply into debt just to get credentials for a profession in which my felony conviction was almost certainly disqualifying. (At 53, to boot.) Why this day was different, I can't say for sure. All I know is that I was driving up to Runyon Canyon with Gaza, and I told myself that if I heard the ad again on the way down I would call and go to an information session. I did hear it again, so I went. I applied, was accepted, and started classes a month later.

I still couldn't justify taking out so many loans, so I just repeated the same mantra I'd said to myself before going to prison — *there are some people you will meet whom you will later be unable to imagine your life not having met.* This was absolutely true. But on some level I was also thinking that a master's degree would cancel out my time behind bars, or at least rebalance the credits and debits of my life's inventory.

Upon entering the program, I specialized in creative writing and wrote several screenplays, one of which turned into my thesis project. *The Exiled Heart* is the story of a concentration camp survivor living in post-war New York who falls in love with a man who may know the fate of the baby she gave up before the Nazis arrested her.

I had grown up listening to stories of the German occupation of France, of course, and liberally informed my heroine with many elements of my mother's personal history. And although Hannah, the protagonist of my script, lives through an incomparably worse nightmare than I ever endured, I was able to suffuse her character with something we did share — an understanding of how profoundly disorienting it is to survive an experience you never expected to survive.

For the better part of 20 years, I thought I would die, and did not. My future, or at least the idea of one, was gradually yanked away in the first years of the epidemic; and just as unexpectedly it was returned, in dribs and drabs, more than a decade later. During that time I stumbled onto meth, a drug that might have been designed specifically to make the user comfortable with this odd psychic disruption. My conception of time itself was altered — instead of past, present, and future; I thought in terms of now, a few hours from now, and later. In my conflation of instant gratification and living in the moment, speed proved the perfect wingman.

When HIV treatments came on the scene in the late '90s, it became safe to conceive of the future "normally" again, but this conception — which I so took for granted when young — by then felt foreign and strange to me. It was as if I'd pawned most of the contents of my house and moved to an apartment, and when I could finally redeem my furniture, had no place to put it. Only in retrospect have I understood how much space the idea of the rest of our life takes up in our consciousness, in the very neurons of our brain. When that space has contracted, it must be painstakingly expanded again.

In my case, I seem to have required a psychic closure to the part of my life defined by AIDS; a second act curtain to an unexpectedly three-act play. It's the only way I can understand my wholly avoidable descent into the harrowing consequences of my own behavior. Prison, to put it in stark terms, was as close as I could get to death without dying. It's as if the suspense was killing me, and in engineering my downfall, I could finally kill the suspense.

What a nice fantasy it was to imagine that the blog I wrote

in prison with my sister's help needed some tuning up here and there and then a publisher would jump on it. It took me the better part of my first year of freedom to accept that the same words that had worked so well when the author was behind bars completely lacked dramatic urgency when he wasn't. Read in one sitting, the compilation was lumpy and repetitive. "It's like the four-hour rough cut of a documentary that needs to be about 90 minutes long," observed my friend Damian, who was editing a Nabokov anthology. "There's something really good here, but you have to sculpt it down." He emphasized that last part. "You have to sculpt it down."

I knew he was right, but my attempts to do so utterly overwhelmed me. I told myself the experience was too fresh and painful, and what I needed to do was just put it aside for a while and return to it later.

Which I did, every few years. And each time, within several days or even hours of starting on a new iteration, I would find myself pacing the hall like Lady Macbeth, wringing my hands with anxiety. With each passing year I had more distance, but my discomfort in tackling the project seemed to get more acute.

Whatever reasons I gave others, I secretly concluded to myself that I was just lazy. Even after spending hundreds of man-hours getting my degree — an effort requiring the reading of scores of books and the writing of a dozen or so research papers — had you put a gun to my head and asked me what the damn problem was, I would have repeated this explanation as the most likely until the middle of last year.

I was just lazy.

Soon after I got off parole, I helped my mother move from the house I'd grown up in to a newly built Assisted Living condo right on the Hudson River. There was plenty to do there, and her best friends — two French teachers from Mount Vernon —

came by often. My sisters and I flew out about twice a year. My brother Steve came less often, but my mother never went more than two months at most without seeing one of us.

With each visit, the change in her became more and more noticeable. She was increasingly distracted and forlorn, and her memory loss accelerated. She took that very personally, berating herself for not being able to remember things. She seemed to believe that if she only tried harder, she would retrieve the razor-sharp mind she once possessed. (In other words, *if she weren't so lazy.*)

My sister Erica pitched the notion that my mom should sell the condo and come live with her in Chico, a small city just north of Sacramento. My mother rejected the suggestion out of hand, repeating what we'd heard so many times over the years, "I never want to be a burden on my children." When my sister got a divorce soon after, we were finally able to convince my mother that her retirement income would actually be a great help to my sister, who had two young children at home. Finally, she consented.

It was a godsend all around. Our mom was never alone, and my sister could spoil her with care and attention. It was a huge worry off our shoulders, but we were unprepared for how short-lived our relief would be.

In March of 2009, my brother Steven took his own life.

His suicide letter insisted that he feared blindness from a detached retina. But when we discovered a five-year-old receipt for the gun, we knew he'd been planning this for a long time. We were shocked but not entirely surprised. Steven had never, ever been happy, and often made the rest of us very unhappy as well, creating serious rifts in the family. At the time of my arrest, in fact, one of my sisters had not spoken to him for several years. Only coming together to support me ended their long estrangement.

During my incarceration, I was closer to Steve than I'd been in years. I was incredibly grateful for his having taken in my dog, and he sent me newsy little notes about Gaza's mini-adventures, with photos enclosed. Our relationship became distant again in the years after my release, and during a Christmas visit, his obsession over what could have caused his retinal detachment made it impossible to have a rational discussion. I did leave a supportive message on his machine the night before his scheduled surgery, which turned out to be the very night he drove up into the hills of Presidio, where he used his gun for the first and only time.

My initial reaction to his death was rage. How could he do this to my mother, who had already endured the loss of one son? He had made it impossible for her to experience her last years in anything but a near constant state of grief. On this point, of course, I was on extremely shaky ground, and my indignation dissipated soon enough. Anger was no doubt easier for me to feel than loss, even if it seemed like I'd already been mourning Steve for years.

My brother's mental illness had been nobody's fault. He chose to deliver himself from pain he found overwhelming, and that was his right. There was nothing I could do about that now. I could only be the son my mother needed me to be from this point on, the son I always should have been, without interruption.

When I visited her after that, it was often so that Erica could take a well-deserved break. Alone with my mother, I discovered entirely new ways of relating to the woman who'd always been a very close friend as well as a parent. Every morning I would gently wake her. Together we would gradually situate her psychologically and geographically, reducing the intense feeling of displacement that arrived with every new day. I would ask her to retell stories of her youth, always from the canon of those I already knew, so I could fill in the details and help her feel she was remembering them herself. More and more, it was clear large chunks of information had been permanently transferred to my databanks for safekeeping. My sisters and I now held my mother's long-term memory between us.

After her morning tea and tartine, she would move to her chair in the living room and read the paper. It was more ritual than anything else, as she retained less and less of what she read as the months went by. We avoided any television requiring her to follow a plot, which often meant that she settled for the kind of game shows she had always held in contempt as mindless noise. Even the lefty cable news we'd always enjoyed together just generated the same questions along the lines of, "Who is that handsome woman?" (Answer — Rachel Maddow. My mother always seemed to refer to lesbians as "handsome.") Very occasionally, there'd be flashes of the fiery liberal I grew up with. She would mute the TV and ask, "But what is wrong with the Republicans?"

I would tell her about my coursework, my screenplays, my subtitling assignments; often repeating it all the next day. I would ask her what she was thinking of when she stared out the window, and the answer for a long time was, "your brothers." One day her answer changed to "the birdfeeder," and I would see that a lovely hummingbird had indeed been keeping her entertained.

It wasn't that she forgot her sons, but it did seem like she was forgetting to be sad about them. I noticed as well that if I never mentioned my time in prison, neither did she.

I don't know which of the tiny strokes she suffered at the beginning of 2015 finally removed the memory of my imprisonment irrevocably, but it was one small blessing to be had during that last, difficult visit in February. Another was that only one of us knew that the last hug I gave her was our final one.

Her final weeks were spent in a lovely hospice in the perfectly-named town of Paradise, just above Chico. (This is the same town tragically leveled by the 2018 Camp Fire. Paradise hospice still stands.) One of my sisters was always at her bedside. Back in Los Angeles, I didn't know what to do with the overwhelming sense of impending loss, so I started writing a short biographical memoir of the person my mother was before she became my mother. I shared the stories I'd grown up hearing and the stories my sisters and I had drawn from her over the years; alternating between reimagining her life before we were born and sharing how her memories had been transmitted to us differently over the years.

She died peacefully on April 6, 2015 — almost 69 years to the day as her own mother. We didn't have a funeral, as she had donated her body to for scientific research. Instead I posted *La Vie de Simone* online, which Sandra then bound into a beautiful memorial tribute.

Many of the reminiscences I shared in *La Vie de Simone* were pulled from a box my Aunt Françoise had sent me several months earlier, which contained my mother's letters sent during and after the war. I kept them on my desk in the weeks after her death as a sort of soothing talisman. When it was finally time to put the box on a shelf in the closet, I slid them in next to another box containing my letters from prison, which my sister had given me after my release. I took that box down and opened it for the first time since I'd moved into the apartment.

I grabbed an envelope at random, and pulled out one of the first pieces I'd written back in the gay dorms of Los Angeles County Jail, *Ink*. To read the story of what one pen represented to me at that moment — and by extension writing itself — had a greater impact on me than if I'd pulled any other sheaf of papers from that box. (If I was a non-believer in guardian angels before, I am perhaps more of an agnostic now.)

For the first time in years, it wasn't painful to reread my own words, because I no longer had to imagine what it was like for my mother to have read them the first time. That was her final gift to me, to take my shame and guilt with her as she freed herself from this life and moved on to another.

I was finally able to start writing this book — as an act of love for myself, for the men I knew behind bars, and for the redemptive power of creativity.

Where Are They Now?

Derek found it best to take a break from Los Angeles, and lives in a much smaller city up north.

Mack (Jerome Punjab Freeze) and I wrote to each other for seven years. After his release, he reconstructed a life as an addiction counselor in California, and is happily married and still sober.

Earl and I exchanged few letters, but did not stay in touch after his release. I ran into Danny once in the streets of L.A., visibly high but not interested in coming to an A.A. meeting.

Jimmy renewed his relationship with Amber, with whom I was in touch for a time on Facebook. At first, their reunion was a happy one, then Jimmy started to use drugs again and became abusive. Amber found a new job in the Midwest, and moved there permanently. I strongly suspect Jimmy ended back up to prison.

Tim, aka Thumper, wrote me once from Avenal, where he ended up after Delano. Chainsaw had been assigned to the same facility, and supposedly "wasn't such a bad guy, after all." When I wrote back I came out to him, and that was the end of our correspondence. I did Google his name when I was writing the chapter about him, *(May or May Not)* and discovered that he was awaiting trial, along with his girlfriend, for the murder of a wealthy gay man he'd robbed in Palm Springs. A more recent search revealed him as a newly born-again Christian, thanking a prison ministry in Susanville. "I'm in for life" he shares with the newsletter, "but I have hope."

ACKNOWLEDGEMENTS

My sister, Sandra Moreano, was so essential to every part of this experience that she got her very own post-script (following). My other sister, Erica Charlesworth, was indispensable in different ways, but indispensable nonetheless.

The editing skills of Carole Schabow, Christine Schabow and Claudia Keenan, in particular, were crucial in shaping preliminary drafts of the book. A.P. Porter for some valuable last-minute suggestions.

Yelena Skye for helping me keep body (and soul) together, and for her indispensable final edit.

Nathaniel Penn and GQ magazine for rescuing me from obscurity.

I am extremely grateful to those listed below for their love and support, or for just being inspiring to me as writers and artists. (Those who wrote me in prison get an extra thanks, and so their names are bolded.)

David Acuña, Samantha Adams, Bruce Alexander, Tim Bergling, Richard Berry, Sally Bowman, Charles Busch, Kathy Boutry, Drew Brody, Les Cambournacs, Vincent Castellanos, **Henri Chabal, Lucie Chabal, Francoise Chabal, Mireille Chabal, Ellen Chandler,** Michael Cormier, Derek Daniels, David Ebershoff, Mary Degli Espositi, Amy Ferris, Angelo Funicelli, Lannie Garrett, Francoise Grab, Julia Glass, Phyllis Zagortz Gordon, Dale Griner, Liz Goumas, Gabe Gutierrez, Sam Harris, Bill Hayes, Richard Hefner, **Andrea Lauren Herz**, Jerry

Marshall, Tom Jackson, Claudia Keenan, Alaina and Anthony Larsen, Hassan Majd, Melinda Massey, Peter McQuaid, Rosalyn and Grace McWatters, Alex, Keir, and Daniella Moreano, Hakhamanesh Mortezaie, Billy O'Connell, Rich Oravec, Louise Owens, **Nick Pacheco,** Kathy Hepinstall Parks, Les Perdriolles, Jon Priest, Nancy Regalado, Beth and Ken Riches, Mark Rogers, Paula Samuel, Molly Secours, Michael Stewart, Helen Stiller, George Snyder, Cheri, Gina, and Desiree Spriggs, Don Stewart, Shira Tarrant, Amy Tollner, Aaron and Brendan Tukey, Michael Van Essen, Brad Ware, Garris Wimmer, Melinda Wright, Frank Yamrus, **Barbara Zaroff.**

And those no longer with us:

Eric Bean, David Blankenship, Paul Bos, Tony Brown, Fay Marks, Tim Melester, Luke Olmsted, Stephen B. Olmsted, Steve J. Olmsted, Simone Chabal Olmsted, Sheria Reid.

And Gaza, the best dog ever.

P.S.

Dear Mark,

While you were living those 286 days on the inside, I was there on the outside, busy typing your letters to post on the blog and sending you news and packages every day. I was your witness. Unlike you, I didn't write extensively about my own experience. I did, however, learn so very much. I learned that family bonds are covalent*, I learned not to be so judgmental, I learned I didn't have all the answers, and most importantly, I learned how much fun creative play could be. Our strong childhood connection re-emerged during that time and has carried us through all the years since. For this, I will be forever grateful. We have helped each other on countless projects one of which was the launch of my own creative life. As you write in your book, 'There are some people you will meet whom you will later be unable to imagine your life not having met." For me, YOU are one of those people. You returning to your own best self was the best thing that could have happened to me and something I had scarcely thought possible. Today, I honestly cannot imagine a life without you.

Thank you, dear brother.

Love, Sandra

* A covalent bond, also called a molecular bond, is a chemical bond that involves the sharing of electron pairs between atoms. These electron pairs are known as shared pairs or bonding pairs, and the stable balance of attractive and repulsive forces between atoms.

WEBSITES

The book website:
www.lavenderisthenewblack.com

Please feel free to contact him at:
markolmsted@gmail.com

His Facebook page is:
www.facebook.com/OlmstedMark

He has written over 100 pieces for:
www.medium.com

His professional subtitling website is:
www.NuanceTitles.com

Mark's personal blog:
thetrashwhisperer.blogspot.com

Sandra's artwork can be found at her blog:
www.sandramoreano.com

"The Man Who Wouldn't Die" (by Nathaniel Penn) is on:
GQ.com

ABOUT THE AUTHOR

Mark has been a writer since he graduated from NYU School of the Arts in 1980. After over a decade in Manhattan, he moved to California to pursue screenwriting and take care of his brother Luke, who died of AIDS in 1991. Gay and HIV+ himself, Mark self-medicated through the worst of the plague years with crystal meth, which led to a conviction for drug-dealing in 2004 and nine months in prison. *Ink from the Pen* is the story of his time behind bars.

In 2013 Mark received a Master's Degree in Humanities from Mount St. Mary's University with a specialization in Creative Writing.

Mark is a film-subtitler and script doctor in Los Angeles, where he lives with his longtime partner, David.

Made in United States
Troutdale, OR
08/13/2023

12063064R00146